SAP Gateway 2.0 and OData

The Complete SAP Gateway Practical Guide – Learn Fast and Easy How to Develop Complex Services and Integrate Them with SAPUI5 / SAP Fiori

The trademarks that are used are without any consent, and the publication of the trademark is without permission or backing by the trademark owner. All trademarks and brands within this book are for clarifying purposes only and are the owned by the owners themselves, not affiliated with this document.

Table of Contents

Chapter 5: Advanced Implementation of Services for Fiori and SAPUI5 Apps – SAP Gateway 2.0 Features

CREATE_DEEP_ENTITY implementation

GET_EXPANDED_ENTITYSET implementation

Conclusion

Thank you!

Introduction

By exposing SAP Business Suite functionality as REST-based OData services, SAP Gateway enables SAP applications to share data with a wide range of devices, technologies, and platforms in a way that is easy to understand and consume.

Using REST services provides the following advantages:

1. Human readability, you can use your browser to see what data you will get.
2. Stateless applications
3. Use standard HTTP GET, PUT, POST, DELETE, and QUERY operation.
4. The implementations are a black box that will be consumed or deployed. The mandatory requirement is only to know how to call and what to receive.

This step-by-step practical guide will give you the version 1 and version 2 SAP Gateway main aspects that will save you time in your development, design and troubleshooting. In addition, it will also help you on the mobile application development side with SAPUI5.

Let's start!

Chapter 1: What is REST, OData and SAP Gateway?

What is REST?

REST, or REpresentational State Transfer, is an architectural style for providing standards between computer systems on the web, making it easier for systems to communicate with each other.
REST is not a standard but **a set of recommendations** and constraints for RESTful web services that include:

- **Client-Server**. System A makes an HTTP request to a URL hosted by System B, which returns a response.
- **It's identical to how a browser works.** The application makes a request for a specific URL. The request is routed to a web server that returns an HTML page.
- **Stateless**. REST is stateless: the client request should contain all the information necessary to respond to a request. In other words, it should be possible to make two or more HTTP requests in any order and the same responses will be received.
- **Cacheable**. A response should be defined as cacheable or not.
- **Layered**. The requesting client does not need to know whether it's communicating with the actual server, a proxy, or any other intermediary.

REST-compliant systems, often called RESTful systems, are characterized by how they are stateless and separate the concerns of client and server.

It is an alternative to the RPC (Remote Procedure Calls) and Web Services.

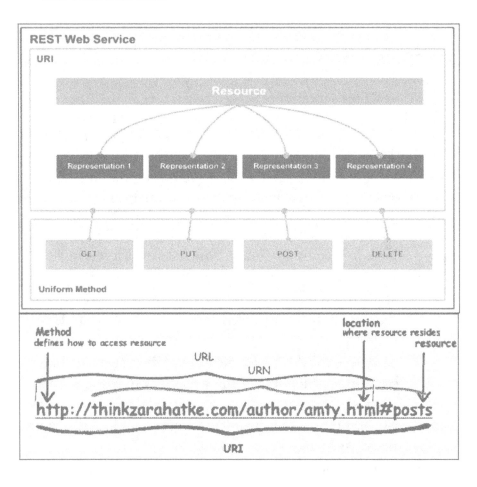

Representations depict parts of the resource state which are transferred between client and server in mostly JSON or XML format.

Client will typically have enough information to manipulate the resource on the server.

For example, if Person is modelled as a resource and there is a service to get contact information of a person then the representation that you will get of that Person would be Name, Address and Phone details in JSON or XML format. Making Requests: REST requires that a client make a request to the server in order to retrieve or modify data on the server.

A request generally consists of:

- an HTTP verb, which defines what kind of operation to perform
- a header, which allows the client to pass along information about the request
- a path to a resource
- an optional message body containing data

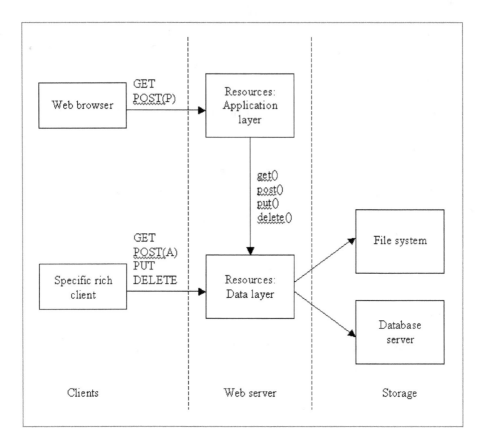

There are 4 basic HTTP verbs we use in requests to interact with resources in a REST system:

- GET — retrieve a specific resource (by id) or a collection of resources
- POST — create a new resource
- PUT — update a specific resource (by id)
- DELETE — remove a specific resource by id

What is OData?

OData is an open data protocol to exchange data over the Internet.

OData or Open Data Protocol is an OASIS standard that defines **a set of best practices for building and consuming RESTful APIs**.

OData helps you focus on your business logic while building RESTful APIs without having to worry about the various approaches to define request and response headers, status codes, HTTP methods, URL conventions, media types, payload formats, query options, etc.

Server hosts the data and clients can call this service to retrieve the resources and manipulate them.

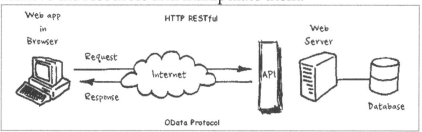

Servers expose one or more endpoints which are services that refers to the resources.

Clients need to know this server-side endpoint to call the service in order to query or manipulate the data.

The **protocol is HTTP based** and designed with **RESTful mindset** which means it follows the constraints to be called as a RESTful service.

Exposing your data with OData service comes with many advantages like for instance, as a consumer, you don't need to worry about the programming language used by the producer as long as the services are exposed as OData services.

What is SAP Gateway?

SAP Gateway is an open standards-based framework to easily connect non-SAP applications, including mobile devices, to SAP applications.

Using the Gateway, developers can connect to SAP applications without knowing how they were made. These applications are just black-boxes and there is no need to use any specific SAP interface/language to call them.

The only needed requirement is leveraging REST services and OData protocol.

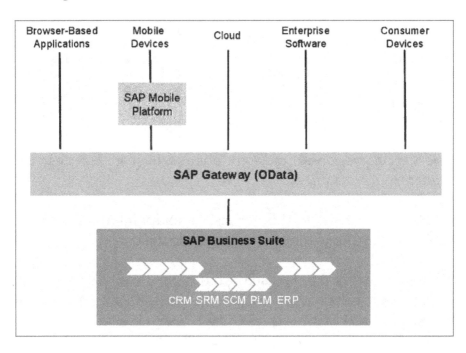

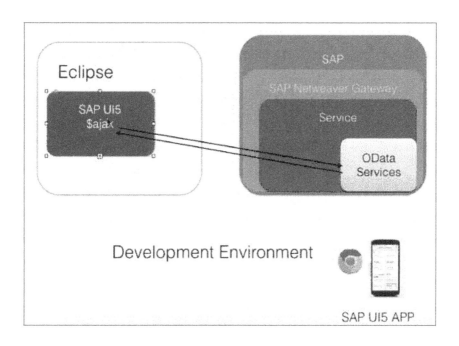

Chapter 2: Getting Familiarized with the Environment

In this section, we will see how SAP NetWeaver Gateway works.

Your SAPUI5 project will be implemented in Eclipse IDE, installed with the SAPUI5 plug-in.

In order to bring data from external applications to the SAPUI5 application, SAP OData services will be triggered by AJAX calls.

These OData services will be responsible for creating, reading or updating the entries in SAP tables.

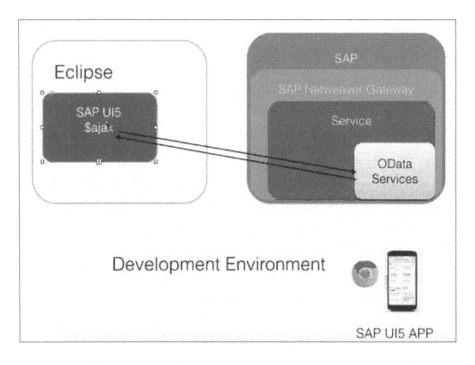

There is a clear separation between the user interface and the backend infrastructure.

Using Gateway in the Application

SAPUI5 front-end applications will run in mobiles, tablets or desktops and the SAPUI5 project will be hosted inside the SAP back-end system, in a Production Environment scenario. The web application will be hosted mainly in front-end devices, but some parts will be on the back-end server side.

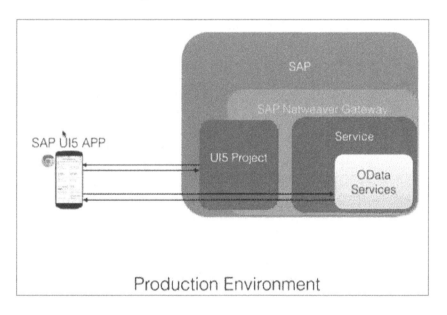

In a nutshell, the SAPUI5 application is not a device-specific app like an Android or IOS app, but it is a hosted application. This hosting is done in the SAP Gateway server.

SAP Gateway is a web application server like Tomcat or Apache server, which basically hosts the application, the SAPUI5 Project, and the web application will run in a client browser or mobile device.

The above picture depicts how a mobile application interacts with the production server, through OData services communication.

Let's now see the main Gateway services and how SAP Gateway is configured.

In order to understand the SAP Gateway, there are three questions to be answered:

- How can we create the services that will be responsible for the OData communication?

- How can we expose these services to the outside world? How can we put them on a web server where anyone can access the data via OData?

- How is testing done for further development? How can we test the services that we just created?

Creation of the services

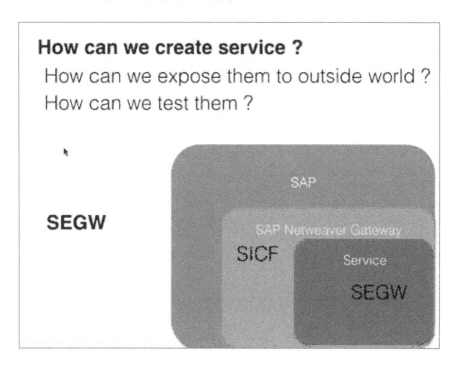

The service creation is done through transaction SEGW - Gateway Service Builder.

T-Code: SEGW

A completely new design-time transaction, which provides developers with an easy-to-use set of tools for creating services. It has been conceived for the code-based OData Channel and supports developers throughout the entire development life cycle of a service.

In Gateway Service Builder, in the left-hand panel, one handles Gateway projects and their related objects, including the final services.

SAP NetWeaver Gateway Service Builder

Project	Description
Z_DEMO_TEST	testing SAP UI5
Z_DEMO_TEST2	testing SAP UI5
ZBAPI_FLIGHT_PROJAM	bapi project
ZBAPI_MULTIPLE_PROJECT	Service using multiple bapi
ZBAPI_MULTIPLE_PROJECT_CODE	project using multiple bapi through coding
ZBMR	myapp
ZDB_PROJECT	project
ZDB_PROJECT_AM	Project Using Custom Table
ZDBPROJECT4	project
ZDBPROJECT5	project
ZFLIGHT_PROJECT_CODE	flight project
ZGWSERVICE	Gateway Service
ZMODEL1	Test
ZPROJECT	Project
ZPROJECT1	ZPROJECT1
ZSALESORDER	SALES ORDER
ZSCN_FLIGHTDEMO	Expose Flight Data
ZTEST	test
ZTEST84	GW Config for Fiori
ZTEST1	test
ZU04_LORD_MY_QUOTATION	Z_User U04 Project

Tutorial Example:

1. Create a project and name the service as "Z_DEMO_TEST3".
2. Write a description, "testing SAP UI5". Give the Package a name. Save it as Local Object.

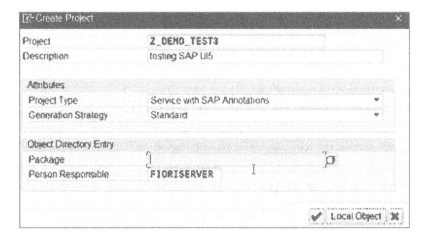

3. In the end, four folders will be created inside the newly created service:
    a. Data Model
    b. Service Implementation
    c. Runtime Artifacts
    d. Service Maintenance

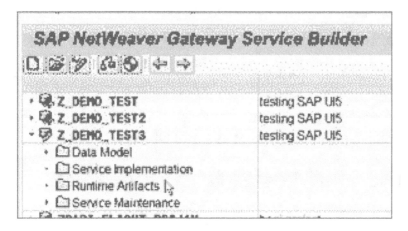

4. Data Model creation

After creating a service, all elements, fields and entities need to be created. It is possible doing it manually or otherwise by browsing tables or RFC/ BAPI functions.

Below is the structure of a custom table "ZUI5_demo_table", for the sake of this example.

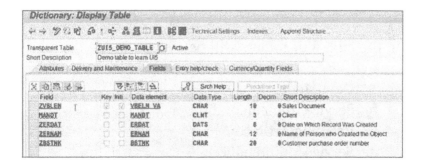

Right-click on Data Model and go to Import the DDIC structure.

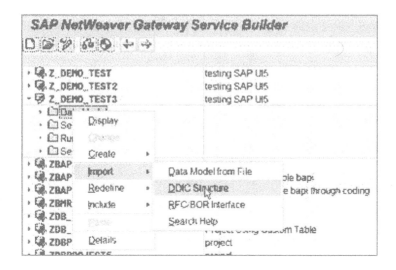

Select "Entity Type" and write the table name, which the service will use, in the Name and ABAP Structure fields.

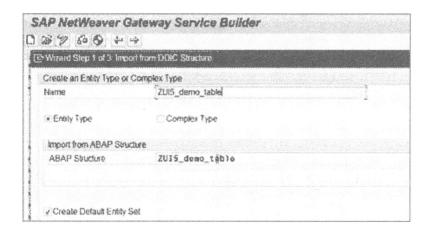

Click Next.

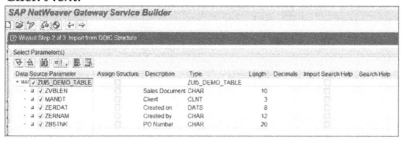

Select all the fields that will be included in the service. Click
Next.

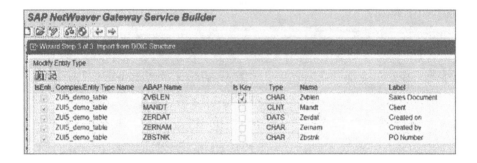

Select the key fields. Make the ZVBLEN as the key. Hit Finish.

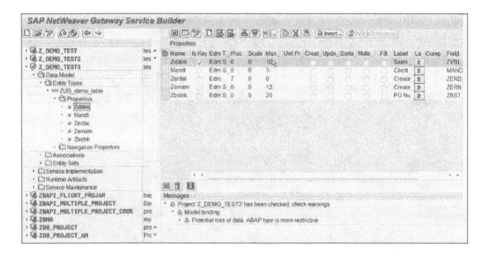

If you expand Data Model, you can see, inside Entity Types,
the Properties, that were added to the "ZUI5_demo_table"
structure, and all their details.
These are the fields that will be used in CRUD service
operations. By marking them, in the checkboxes, we define
what fields are used/allowed in each specific operation:
creation, updating, sorting or filtering.
Save this.

5. Provider classes generation

The next step is to generate the provider classes based on the previous model data design.

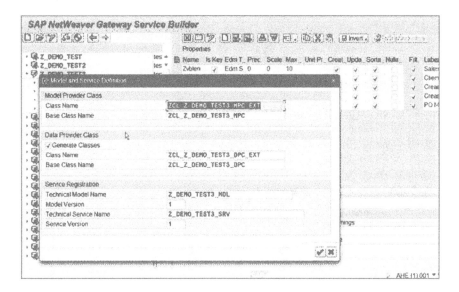

Above, the picture shows the proposal of the classes that will be generated and redefined afterwards, if needed. For each service call, there will be an ABAP call to the relevant method, in order to implement the custom solution and return the specific service HTTP response.

After the generation, inside Runtime Artifacts folder, new files have been created.

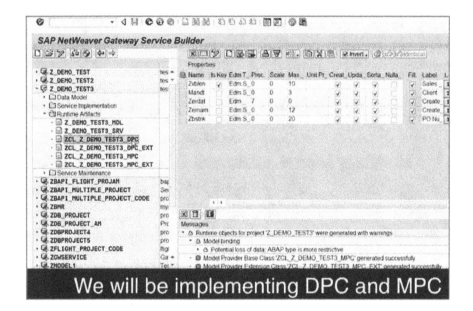

We will be implementing DPC and MPC

DPC stands for Data Provider Class and the MPC stands for Model Provider Class.

DPC_EXT and MPC_EXT classes will have the custom code that will handle the service calls.

Testing the services before DPC and MPC custom development

Before testing the service, it is needed to register it under Service Maintenance folder. Technical Service Name is the name of our service. Assign this as a Local Object.
Click on Continue.
Go to Maintain, that redirects to the Activate and Maintain Services transaction, /IWFND/MAINT_SERVICE .

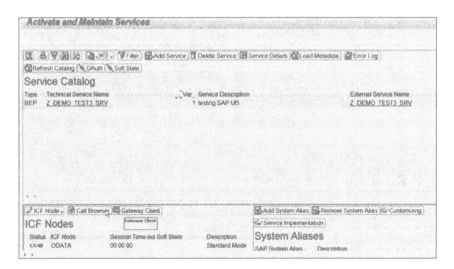

Under ICF Nodes, there is the status of the service. Green-colored status means this can be reached from outside SAP via web browser.

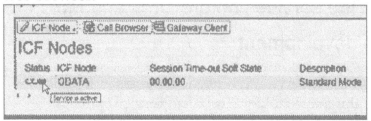

In order to test the service, use first the Gateway Client. Click Execute. Under HTTP Response, on the right panel, the results are shown. The HTTP status code 200 means the response was successful.

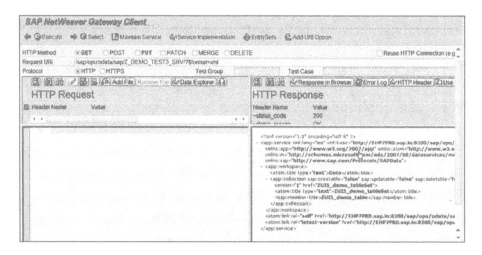

To turn the response more readable, there is the JSON option, by appending *?$format=json* at the end of the URL.

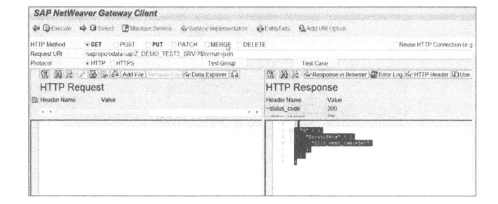

After using the Gateway Client, one can also test with the browser. After inserting the credentials, SAP user and password, the results will be displayed.

In order to get metadata information i.e. all fields involved in the services and basic information, $metadata keyword should be used after service name.

Going back and reviewing what has been done:

1. Creation of services
2. Data elements and entities involved in the services
3. Directly importing all entities from Z structure
4. Registration of the service
5. Testing the service

Publishing the services

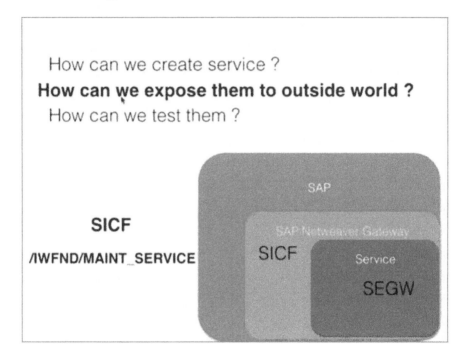

How can we create service ?

How can we expose them to outside world ?

How can we test them ?

SICF

/IWFND/MAINT_SERVICE

SAP

SAP Netweaver Gateway

SICF

Service

SEGW

In order to tell the SAP system to expose the services to the outside world, SICF transaction is required.

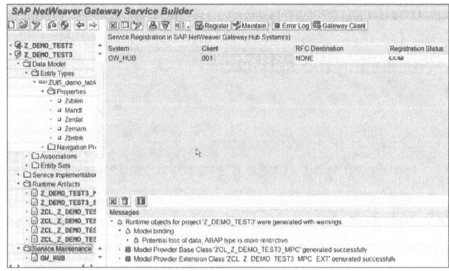

Open SICF transaction and under Service Name, search for Z_* to find Z_DEMO_TEST3_SRV service.

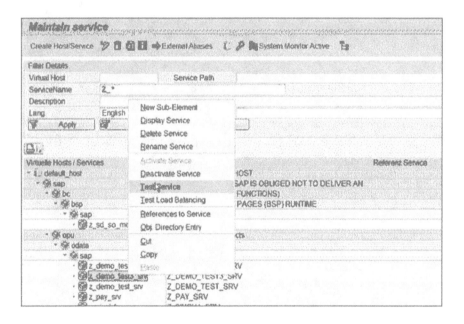

Z_DEMO_TEST3_SRV is already activated since previously we executed that step by going to SEGW transaction and, within Service Maintenance folder, directly registered it and activated it.

In SICF, it is possible to switch on/off any service and therefore allowing or not allowing its execution.

If one needs to open the service maintenance transaction directly and not doing it through SEGW transaction, the code is /IWFND/MAINT_SERVICE.

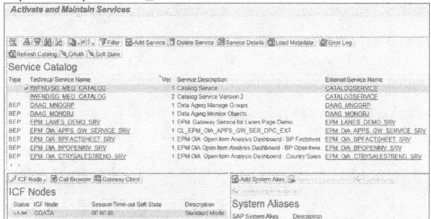

This /IWFND/MAINT_SERVICE transaction cockpit is the core maintenance point where several service actions can be performed.

1. Activation/deactivation of ICF nodes to activate or stop services
2. Running the Gateway client or the external browser to test services
3. Adding new services and new system aliases
4. Checking error logs while developing the services

Implementing service handling through DPC and MPC

For now, in the web browser, all you can see is the metadata and the basic service information, no specific service implementation has been implemented yet.

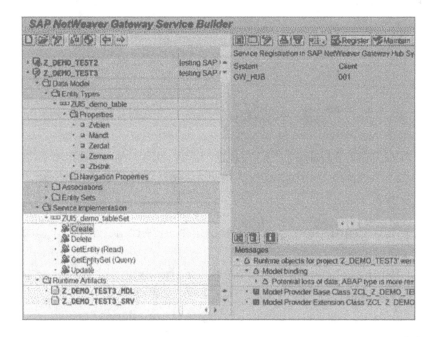

In SAP Gateway Service Builder - SEGW transaction, within Service Implementation folder ZUI5_demo_tableSet, there are all CRUD operations: CREATE, READ, UPDATE and DELETE data.

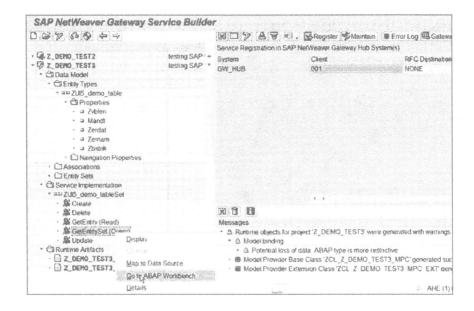

Let us first implement the GetEntititySet. which is the READ operation.

It is like a SELECT * that gives all the results from a table with all of the fields you have defined.

Right-click on GetEntitySet and go to ABAP Workbench. Save the project.

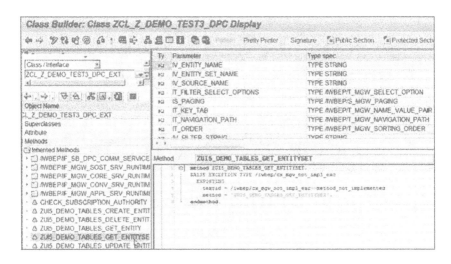

In Class Builder, inside Inherited Methods we can see the
GetEntitySet method. Right-click on GetEntitySet then
Redefine, and it will open the method in edit mode.

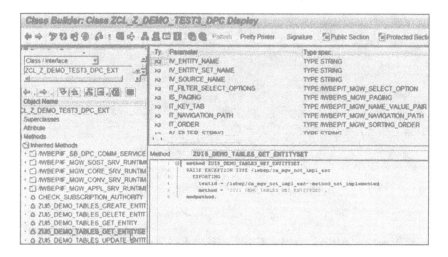

There are several import parameters from where it is possible
to pass some of the filtering criteria, but the focus should be at
the ET_ENTITYSET export parameter which is the body of the
response, the HTTP response that will show up in the return
browser page.

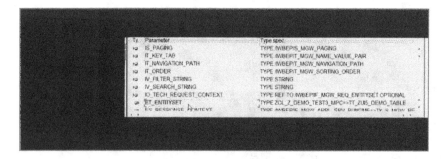

Let's implement ET_ENTITYSET with a very basic SELECT *.

```
SELECT * FROM ZUI5_DEMO_TABLE into CORRESPONDING FIELDS
OF TABLE ET_ENTITYSET.
```

Save it and check if things are correct and activate all the objects.

In the web browser, after opening ZUI5_demo_tableSet, we can see the result data in XML format.

In JSON format the result is more readable.

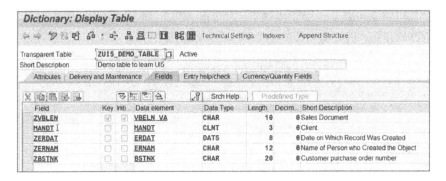

The SAPUI5 application will execute AJAX calls and will get and display JSON objects like the example above.

This is a basic GetEntitySet, a simple SELECT *, for the sake of this initial example, but can be more complex and detailed if we use filter criteria or other queries like $top or $skip.

The DPC implementation, in the Class Builder, will implement the queries.

For instance, for the query $top=2, it is expected to be displayed only 2 records. Since there is no specific implementation yet in this case, the HTTP response will return all four records. In the DPC class, will be required therefore to implement the query or filtering criteria, if needed.

In the next section, we will see more about service implementation like creating, registering and activating the services.

Summary

In this section, we saw the architecture of SAP Gateway system, how we can we use it to build an application on top of it and how SAPUI5 interacts with it.

We also answered three main questions:

1. How can we create services?
2. How can we expose them to outside world?
3. How can we test them?

To answer these questions, we went inside the SAP Gateway system in order to understand how it is structured.

We also understood all the details we need consider while building a service, like transaction codes, how a basic service is created and exposed, how they are accessed from the internet and how to build those services.

At the end, we implemented our first service where we were able to read multiple records of an SAP table.

Wow! Congratulations!

Do you know that **67%** of the readers **don't finish** the book they are reading and that a relevant percentage **don't even start the second chapter**?
You are on the good track to finish this useful practical guide and my family and I congratulate you for this! :)

In fact, this book is fully practical with no fluff and I spent many cups of coffee to put it together.
Hope you like it and please leave a review in order to help me as an author and to improve the content of this book.
Your review is very important. I will read it very carefully as it will be used as a tool to refine my work! Thank you!
<u>CLICK HERE TO LEAVE FEEDBACK ON AMAZON</u>
If you're undecided, just leave the review later...
Ah! By the way, this photo was taken last Summer in Amsterdam. Very hot day! :)

Chapter 3: CRUDQ operations and service implementation

In this section, we will focus on CRUD operations.

What is a CRUD Operation?

Sometimes, it is also referred as CRUDQ and stands for Create-Read-Update-Delete, and Q for Query.
C.R.U.D.Q

- C:Create
- R:Read
- U:Update
- D:Delete
- Q:Query

Create a Service for CRUDQ Operations

The backend table for the operations will be the
ZUI5_DEMO_TABLE table below.

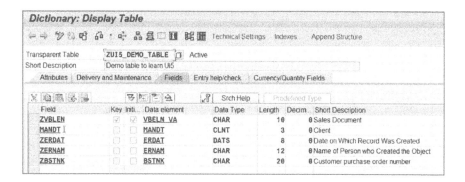

The final SAPUI5 application, in the next chapter, will execute
AJAX calls that will maintain the backend data (create, read,
update, delete or query records) via Gateway services.
This table has a few records for testing purposes.

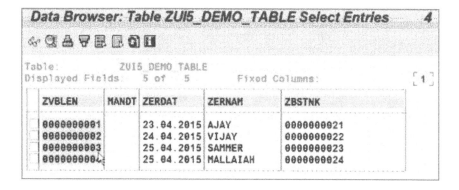

Let's see how those operations can be done via SAP Gateway.

In SEGW transaction, create a new service, Z_DEMO_TEST4, put in the description and the package as $TMP. Click on the check button to create the projects where the services will be implemented.

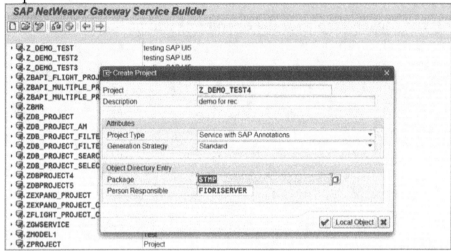

The first step is to import the ZUI5_DEMO_TABLE structure with which the services will be dealing.

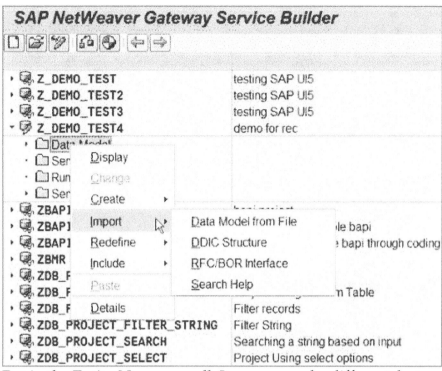

Put in the Entity Name as well. Its name can be different, but for the sake of the example, it will be equal to the table structure in order to be easier to identify. Press next.

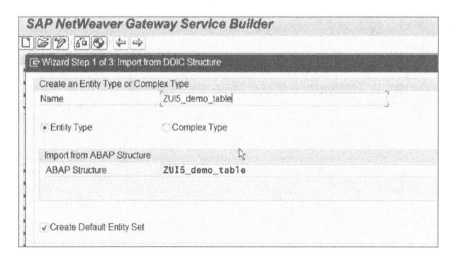

Select all parameters and click Next.

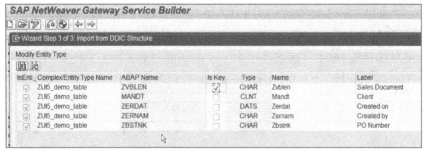

We must mention which is the key field: ZVBLEN. Hit Finish and Save.

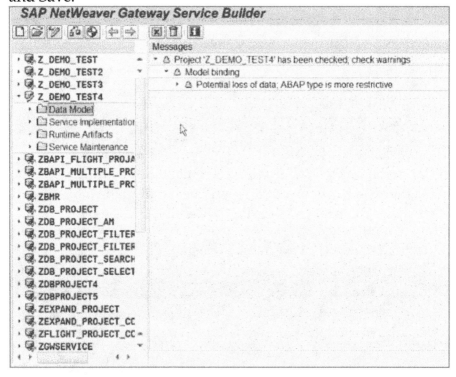

We have imported the structure that will be used by the services. Under Data Model, inside Entity Types, we can find the structure and its individual properties.

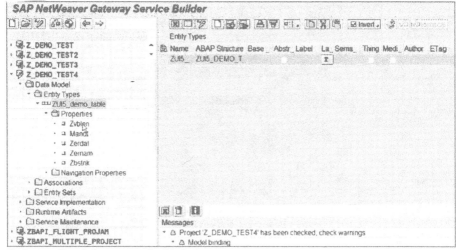

Select all of them and click Insert.

Above, we flag the Create and Update columns that will say to the Gateway service that these entities can be created or updated.

Next, we go to the project and Generate Runtime Objects in order to generate the Model Provider Class and Data Provider Class.

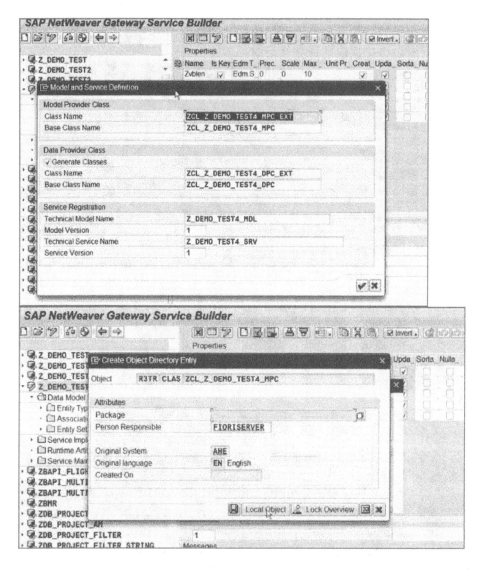

Now that the runtime objects have been generated, we can find them inside Runtime Artifacts, both DPC and MPC extensions.

DPC extension class is where the services are created and used through the browser.

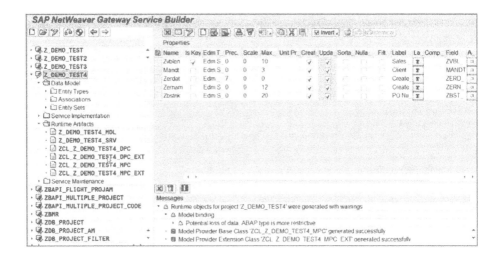

The next thing to do is going to the Gateway Cockpit, from the Service Maintenance folder, and register the service by giving the technical names.

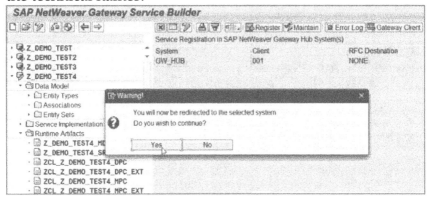

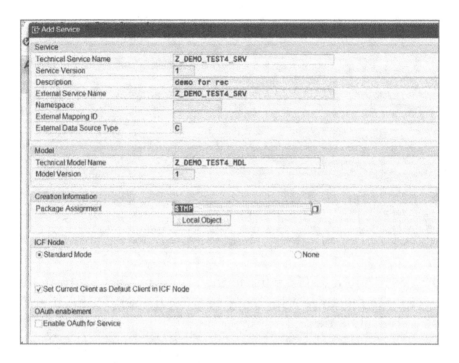

After registering the service, you go to maintenance and see if the service is running fine.

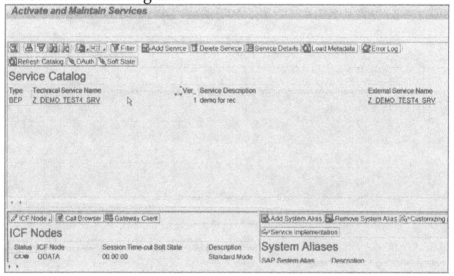

The service has been automatically selected and we can see that the OData node is active as the status is green. We can now go to the Gateway client or to the browser to test the services.

By pressing Execute, the result is returned with HTPP status code 200 (OK).

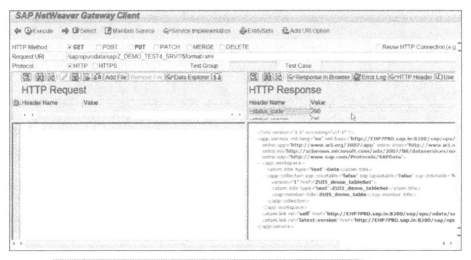

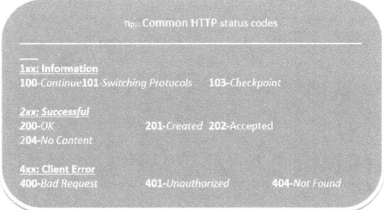

The services have been successfully registered and therefore we can start implementing the CRUD operations in the service builder (SEGW transaction).

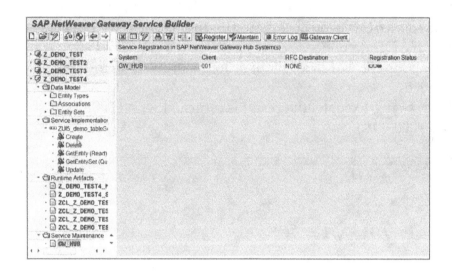

Query operation

The first operation we will implement is Query.
Right-click on the DPC_EXT Runtime Artifact and go to ABAP Workbench.

C:Create R:Read U:Update D:Delete **Q:Query**

GET

Go inside Methods. Inside Inherited Methods there are 5 methods that will be implemented in the following sections.

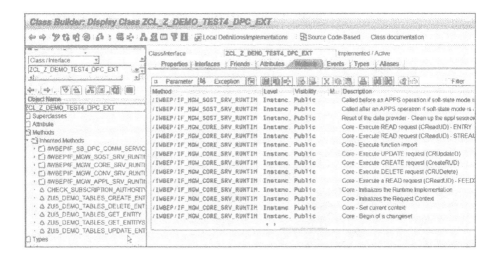

The first method is the GET_ENTITYSET related method, where the record selection will be implemented: the ZUI5_DEMO_TABLES_GET_ENTITYSET method.

This generated method name comes from the concatenation of the Z structure name ZUI5_DEMO_TABLES and the method type GET_ENTITYSET.

Right-click ZUI5_DEMO_TABLES_GET_ENTITYSET and press Redefine.

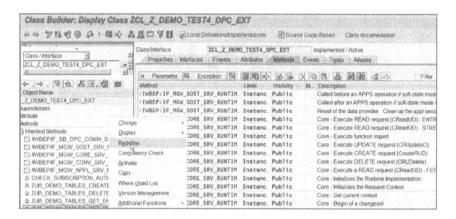

Between the several import, export and exception method parameters, there is the payload HTTP return ET_ENTITYSET.

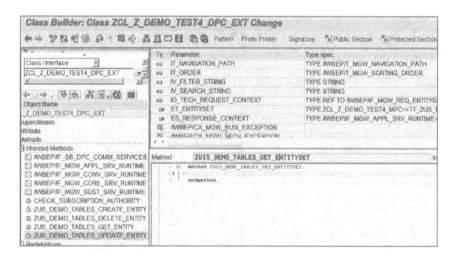

The example ABAP code for the query operation will be:

```
SELECT * on the ZUI5_DEMO_TABLE into CORRESPONDING
FIELDS OF TABLE ET_ENTITYSET.
```

ET_ENTITYSET is the export parameter with the same structure of ZUI5_DEMO_TABLES table. The code selects all data and moves it to ET_ENTITYSET.

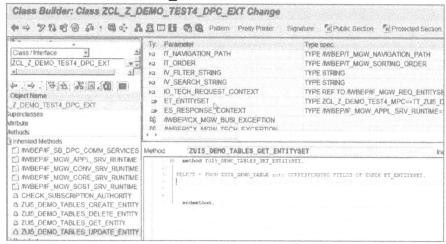

Save the method GET_ENTITYSET and activate it.

In the Gateway Client, test the service with the following URL:
```
/sap/opu/odata/sap/Z_DEMO_TEST4_SRV/ZUI5_demo_tableSet/
?$format=json
```

- `Z_DEMO_TEST4_SRV` is the name of the service
- `ZUI5_demo_tableSet` is how the service recognizes the name of the method
- `?$format=json` specifies the output format
-

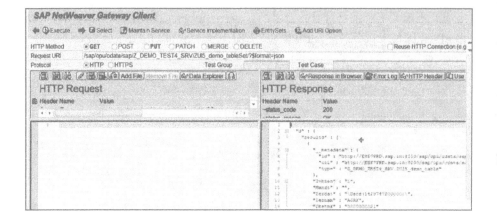

The HTTP method is the GET verb since it is a reading operation.

After pressing Execute, we will get all records of the table.

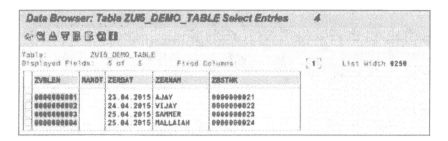

The same thing can be done in your web browser. The difference from the Gateway client, is that the host name and the port number should also be supplied.

```
{
  - d: {
    - results: {
      - {
        - __metadata: {
            id: "http://ehp7prd.sap.in:8200/sap/opu/odata/sap/Z_DEMO_TEST4_SRV/ZUI5_demo_tableSet('1')",
            uri: "http://ehp7prd.sap.in:8200/sap/opu/odata/sap/Z_DEMO_TEST4_SRV/ZUI5_demo_tableSet('1')",
            type: "Z_DEMO_TEST4_SRV.ZUI5_demo_table"
          },
          Zvblen: "1",
          Mandt: "",
          Zerdat: "/Date(1429747200000)/",
          Zernam: "AJAY",
          Zbatnk: "0000000021"
        },
      - {
        - __metadata: {
            id: "http://ehp7prd.sap.in:8200/sap/opu/odata/sap/Z_DEMO_TEST4_SRV/ZUI5_demo_tableSet('2')",
            uri: "http://ehp7prd.sap.in:8200/sap/opu/odata/sap/Z_DEMO_TEST4_SRV/ZUI5_demo_tableSet('2')",
            type: "Z_DEMO_TEST4_SRV.ZUI5_demo_table"
          },
          Zvblen: "2",
          Mandt: "",
          Zerdat: "/Date(1429839600000)/",
          Zernam: "VIJAY",
          Zbatnk: "0000000022"
        },
      - {
        - __metadata: {
            id: "http://ehp7prd.sap.in:8200/sap/opu/odata/sap/Z_DEMO_TEST4_SRV/ZUI5_demo_tableSet('3')",
            uri: "http://ehp7prd.sap.in:8200/sap/opu/odata/sap/Z_DEMO_TEST4_SRV/ZUI5_demo_tableSet('3')",
            type: "Z_DEMO_TEST4_SRV.ZUI5_demo_table"
```

Gateway client testing should be done first, before the browser testing, since it is a faster procedure.

Read operation

C:Create **R:Read** U:Update D:Delete **Q:Query**

GET

When there is a need to read specific data records and not a set of data or all data, the READ operation is the most suitable.

In the below example, one single record with key value '2' will be read through the GET_ENTITY method.

The GET_ENTITYSET is used to read sets of records and the GET_ENTITY method is used to read specific records.

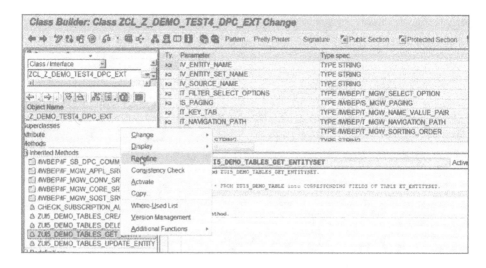

Go to Class Builder, right-click on GET_ENTITY, and redefine it. Test example is below.

```
DATA:lv_vbeln TYPE vbak-vbeln,
ls_key_tab TYPE /iwbep/s_mgw_name_value_pair.
*Get the key property values
READ TABLE it_key_tab INTO ls_key_tab WITH KEY name 'Zvblen'.
SELECT single *"ZVBELN MANDT ZERDAT ZERNAM ZBSTNK
from ZUI5_demo_table into CORRESPONDING FIELDS OF er_entity where
zvblen eq ls_key_tab-value.
if sy-subrc <>0."Throw exception here ENDIF.
```

Some importing parameters are critical in this scenario such as the key values table.

For instance, if we want to read the second record, we should pass the value, in the URL, so that we can filter the table with it. The IT_KEY_TAB importing parameter will have all the key values that are passed via URL.

```
/sap/opu/odata/sap/Z_DEMO_TEST4_SRV/ZUI5_demo_tableSet(
'0000000002')
```

The above code processes the URL call in the following way:

- Retrieves the value that has been passed in the URL, by reading the import table with its key field ZVBLEN: *READ TABLE it_key_tab INTO ls_key_tab WITH KEY name 'zvblen'.*

- Once the value is retrieved, it can be used in the any operation. In this example, the key value is used to select all its details: *SELECT single * from ZUI5_demo_table into CORRESPONDING FIELDS OF er_entity where zvblen eq ls_key_tab-value.*

Save this code, activate, and put an external debugging point.

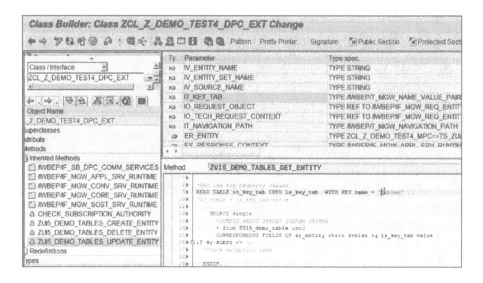

Go to the Gateway Client and insert the URL:
`/sap/opu/odata/sap/Z_DEMO_TEST4_SRV/ZUI5_demo_tableSet(`
`'0000000002')`

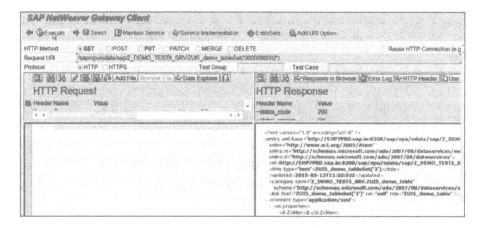

Press Execute and it will stop at the debugging point.

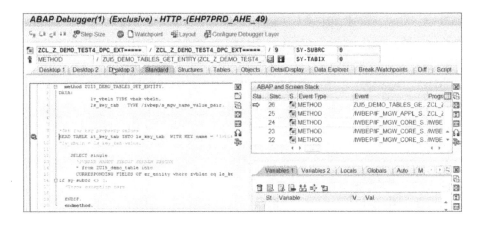

If we inspect IT_KEY_TAB, we can see that it has one value, the one that was passed in the URL.

The table has the structure

/wbep/s_mgw_name_value_pair and has 3 columns: Column 1 is Row, Column 2 is a CString value called NAME, and Column 3 is also a CString value called VALUE. Zvblen is the key of the table and the value that was passed via URL is the 0000000002.

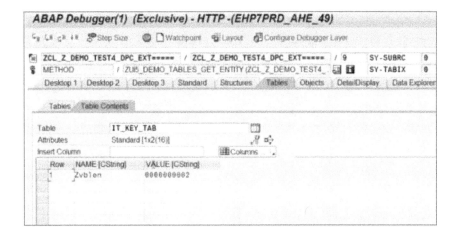

The relevant value from the internal table is copied to a local structure ls_key_tab.

The value field of the structure, `ls_key_tab-value`, contains the value of the URL, `0000000002` that will be used in the select statement.

After the operation, the `sy-subrc` value will be zero and the result will populate `er_entity` object. If it is not zero, you can throw an exception that will be reflected in the service, and the relevant error message will be shown.

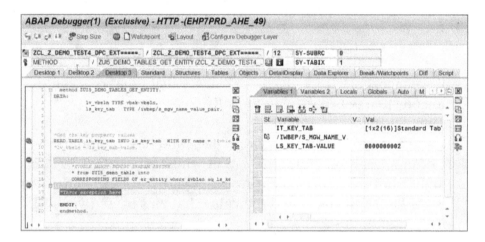

The value inside `er_entity` will be the single record that was read, and which will be exported.

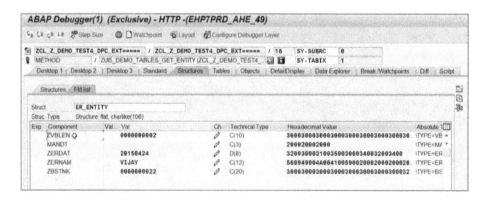

```
/sap/opu/odata/sap/Z_DEMO_TEST4_SRV/ZUI5_demo_tableSet(
'0000000002')
```

To finish this section, bear in mind you can have multiple keys as well, separated by a comma, so that your `ls_key_tab` will have multiple records.

Create operation

This operation is used to create new records in the table, and the HTTP POST operation of the HTTP AJAX request will be used in this scenario.

To implement it, we go back to the Class Builder and select CREATE_ENTITYSET method. Right-click and select Redefine.

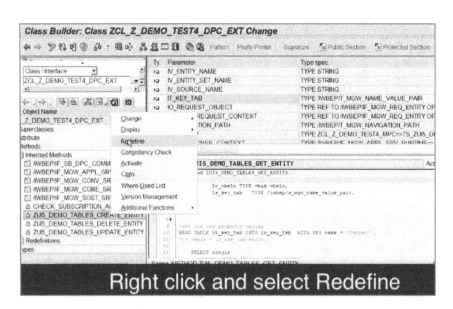

Let's paste the ABAP code below:

```
DATA: ls_request_input_data TYPE
ZCL_Z_DEMO_TEST3_MPC=>TS_ZUI5_DEMO_TABLE,
ls_userinfo TYPE ZUI5_DEMO_TABLE.
* Read Request Data
io_data_provider->read_entry_data( IMPORTING es_data =
ls_request_input_data ).
* Fill workarea to be inserted
ls_userinfo-ZVBLEN = ls_request_input_data-ZVBLEN.
ls_userinfo-ZERDAT = ls_request_input_data-ZERDAT.
ls_userinfo-ZERNAM = ls_request_input_data-ZERNAM.
ls_userinfo-ZBSTNK = ls_request_input_data-ZBSTNK.
* Insert Data in table ZUSERINFO
INSERT ZUI5_DEMO_TABLE FROM ls_userinfo.
IF sy-subrc = 0.
er_entity = ls_request_input_data. "Fill Exporting parameter
ER_ENTITY
ENDIF.
```

The data in the HTTP POST payload will be provided to the
code through the object `IO_DATA_PROVIDER` and will be
copied to the work area `ls_request_input_data`.

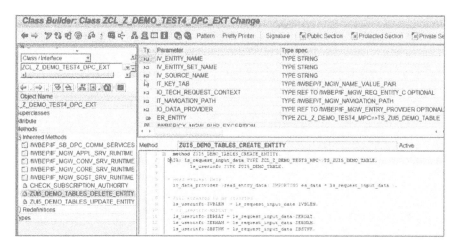

Once we get the values, we move the data to the
`ls_userinfo` structure and call the `INSERT` statement.
Afterwards we return the data as an HTTP answer by moving
the data to the export object parameter `er_entity`.

Let's run this method using the Gateway client. In order to get the data of a record or row, we must use the GET_ENTITY that has been created in the previous section.

Press execute and click on button *Use As Request* (as shown in below image) that will copy the response data to the left panel of the Gateway client.

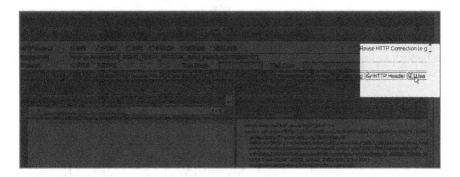

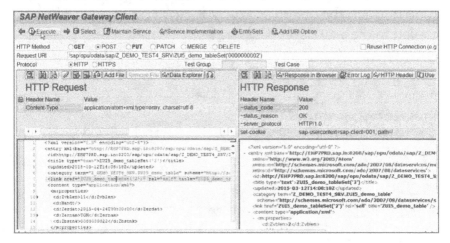

Let us proceed to create a new record by editing the payload.

```
<?xml version="1.0" encoding="utf-8"?>
<entry xml:base="http://EHP7FRD.sap.in:8200/sap/opu/odata/sap/Z_DEM
  <id>http://EHP7FRD.sap.in:8200/sap/opu/odata/sap/Z_DEMO_TEST4_SRV/2
  <title type="text">ZUI5_demo_tableSet('2')</title>
  <updated>2015-03-12T14:06:18Z</updated>
  <category term="Z_DEMO_TEST4_SRV.ZUI5_demo_table" scheme="http://s
  <link href="ZUI5_demo_tableSet('2')" rel="self" title="ZUI5_demo_t
  <content type="application/xml">
    <m:properties>
      <d:Zvblen>?</d:Zvblen>
      <d:Mandt/>
      <d:Zerdat>2015-04-14T00:00:00</d:Zerdat>
```

T-Code: /IWFND/ERROR_LOG

The Error Log for SAP NetWeaver Gateway hub systems is a helpful addition to the existing Application Log Viewer and provides detailed context information about errors that have occurred at runtime.

While performing the operation, there were some errors, and the error 'Method Not Allowed' was triggered. In order to investigate the causes, we will jump to the error troubleshooting transaction /IWFND/ERROR_LOG.

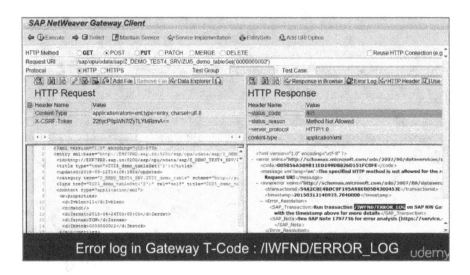

Error log in Gateway T-Code : /IWFND/ERROR_LOG

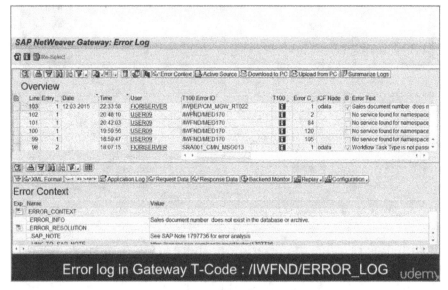

Error log in Gateway T-Code : /IWFND/ERROR_LOG

The log says that the provided data does not exist in the archive. The reason for the error is the wrong non-required parameter that was being used in the URL. Get rid of it and execute again.

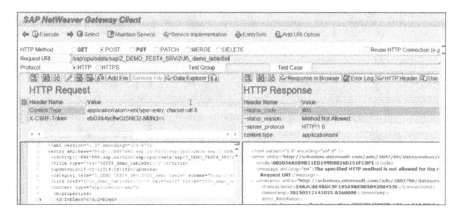

`/sap/opu/odata/sap/Z_DEMO_TEST4_SRV/ZUI5_demo_tableSet`

In HTTP POST method, in Creation, the data is passed in the payload and not in the URL.

One of the important things when we do an AJAX call via SAPUI5 application is that you also must give the X-CSRF-Token. X-CSRF-Token is automatically copied in the response when the data is used as request, but when we are calling from the SAPUI5 application we must manually give the X-CSRF-Token.

This is used to prevent forgeries and it is a security mechanism for the web services to accept data only from legitimate sources.

When you do a GET call, you automatically get an X-CSRF-Token, which will be used via POST request as well.

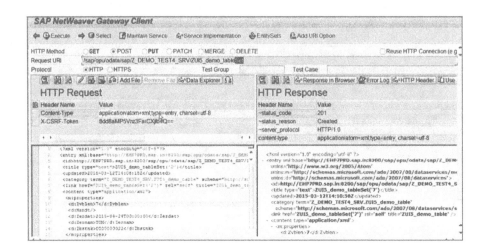

If we are doing this with a web browser, to do a GET request for the first time, the Gateway will ask for credentials, so the security is maintained via service calls.

Update operation

C:Create R:Read U:Update D:Delete **Q:Query**

PUT

In this Update scenario, we will read the data entry in object
IO_DATA_PROVIDER and use the *UPDATE* ABAP statement.
We will also debug the program so that you can see what is
going on inside the ABAP code.
In order to implement it, we go back to the Class Builder and
select UPDATE_ENTITYSET method. Right-click and select
Redefine.

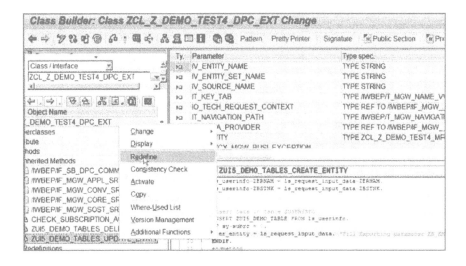

Let's paste the code below.

```
DATA: ls_request_input_data TYPE
zcl_z_demo_test3_mpc=>ts_zui5_demo_table,
ls_userinfo TYPE zui5_demo_table.
* Read Request Data
io_data_provider->read_entry_data( IMPORTING es_data =
ls_request_input_data ).
" Update fields of table ZUSERINFO
UPDATE zui5_demo_table SET
zvblen = ls_request_input_data-zvblen
zerdat = ls_request_input_data-zerdat
zernam = ls_request_input_data-zernam
zbstnk = ls_request_input_data-zbstnk
where zvblen= ls_request_input_data-zvblen.
IF sy-subrc= 0.
er_entity = ls_request_input_data.
ENDIF.
```

Save it, and then Activate.

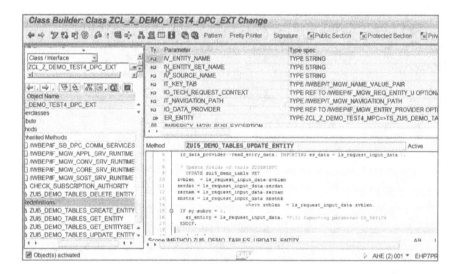

Below, we can see that the entry record '7' created in the previous section.

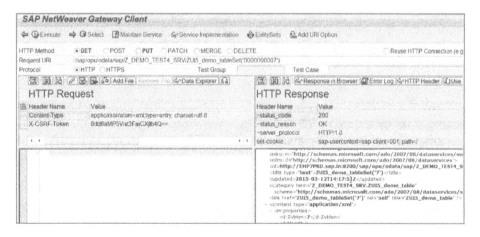

ZVBLEN	MANDT	ZERDAT	ZERNAM	ZBSTNK
0000000001		23.04.2015	AJAY	0000000021
0000000002		24.04.2015	VIJAY	0000000022
0000000003		25.04.2015	SAMMER	0000000023
0000000004		25.04.2015	MALLAIAH	0000000024
0000000007		24.04.2015	TOM	0000000022

In this scenario, we will update this created entry, and we will change the name of TOM to JERRY.

To test your Call Update, let's go the to Gateway client.

First, we must read the record so that we can update it: do a *Read* operation to get the records and use the response XML body as a request again.

```
/sap/opu/odata/sap/Z_DEMO_TEST4_SRV/ZUI5_demo_tableSet(
'0000000007')
```

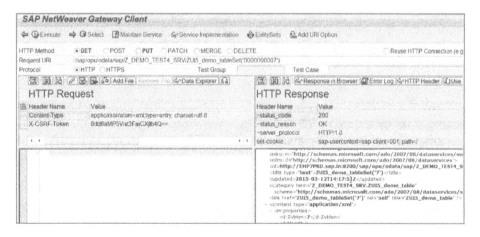

You can see the HTTP Response above and the XML as the response body. Click on *Use As Request*, to use the same response as a request. This will copy the payload to the left panel.

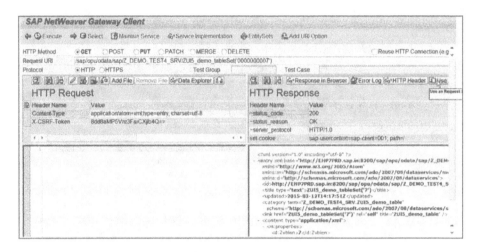

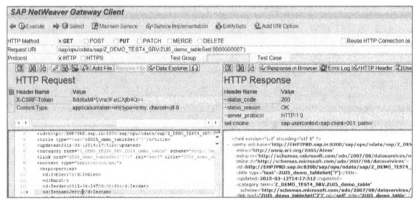

On the left side of the Gateway Client, we edit the HTTP request content, that will be sent to the server, and change the name to 'JERRY'.

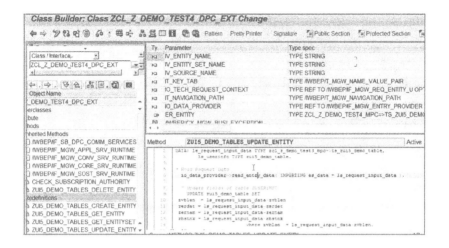

With the data that is passed in the body, the program reads the relevant record, copies it to the local structure `ls_request_input_data` and updates DB table `zui5_demo_table` accordingly, where `ZVBLEN` key table field is equal to the record.

For Update actions, the HTTP method to be used should be PUT. After executing the call, the database record is updated, and the client returns a successful response with a 204 status.

We have successfully implemented the Update operation and let us now put a debugging point to show you the program working. Go to Gateway client and set an external breakpoint in the update entity method.

The `read_entry_data` method reads the payload into the structure *ls_request_input_data.*

By inspecting the structure variable *ls_request_input_data,* we can see the record with *'Jerry02'.*

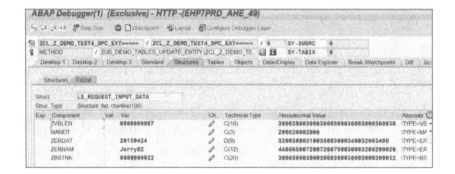

Afterwards, we update the database table with record that has been read.

The HTTTP status code 204 tells us that the operation was successful.

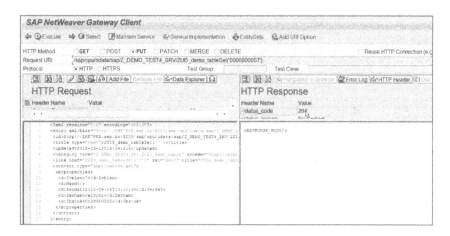

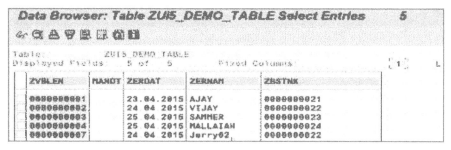

Delete operation

C:Create R:Read U:Update D:Delete Q:Query

DELETE

For the Delete operation we read the same table, as we did for the Read operation, getting the key records and delete the relevant entries.
Go to Class Builder and Redefine the Delete method.

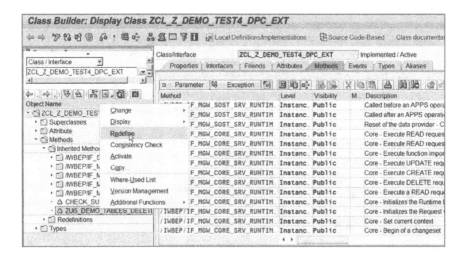

Let's paste the code below.

```
DATA: ls_key_tab TYPE /iwbep/s_mgw_name_value_pair,
lv_vblen TYPE ZUI5_DEMO_TABLE-ZVBLEN.
* Read key values
READ TABLE it_key_tab INTO ls_key_tab WITH KEY name = 'Zvblen'.
lv_vblen = ls_key_tab-value.
IF lv_vblen IS NOT INITIAL.
DELETE FROM ZUI5_DEMO_TABLE WHERE zvblen = lv_vblen.
ENDIF.
```

Save and Activate it.

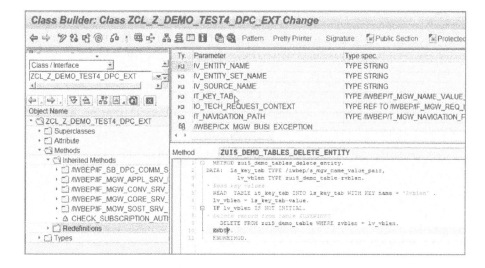

Zvblen is the key we read, and according to that key value, we will delete the record from the zui5_demo_table. The sy-subrc check can be used after the database deletion, to throw an exception in case of any error.

In the Gateway client, we call a GET to bring the record with key 7.

```
/sap/opu/odata/sap/Z_DEMO_TEST4_SRV/ZUI5_demo_tableSet(
'0000000007')
```

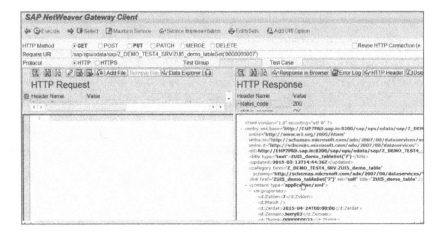

Now in order to delete this record, we select the HTTP Method DELETE, instead of GET.

By executing it, we get a 204 status successful message. The 200 series of response messages are all successful messages. This means the operation was executed successfully and the record with key 7 should have been deleted.

Let us check.

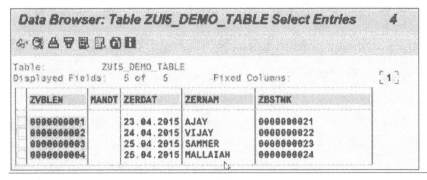

One way to check if the operation has been successful is by doing one more Read operation for that record to check if the record has been deleted. As we can see below, the client returned a 404 error status for this Read operation.

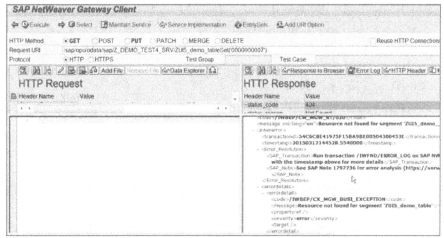

We have now successfully implemented the CRUDQ operations.

In the next section, we will expose these operations, via SAP Gateway, to the outside world, in order they can be used in an SAPUI5/Fiori application.

Summary

In this section, we have seen CRUDQ operations, Create, Read, Update, Delete, and Query.
We have implemented each one of them in the SAP Gateway system step-by step and have tested them in both ways: Gateway client and web browser.
We have also come to know the authentication mechanism for the Gateway system while accessing the service from the internet.
In the next section, we will see these CRUDQ operations with an SAPUI5 app.
The procedure to access these services will be a bit different with SAPUI5 app, so we will go into details of how to use the services we have just created in the SAPUI5 app.

Chapter 4: Integrating with SAPUI5 and deploying app

In this section, we will see how to implement the CRUD operations inside the SAPUI5 application.

Basic setup for SAPUI5 CRUD App

In the previous section, we saw how to create the CRUD operations and how to test them with the SAP Gateway Client.

We have also tested the operations with a browser, but not the methods Create, Update and Delete. The reason for this is because creating those scenarios using AJAX calls is a complicated task as there are some security exceptions which we must deal with.

There are several classes present inside the library which will make this task lot easier, and therefore it will be the go-to method to use the Create, Update and Delete methods inside the SAPUI5 application.

Let's see the Gateway Client to see the Update, Create and Delete processes and where we copied the data.

For example, if we retrieve the details using the GET method, we can use the response as the request and afterwards we can change the input values in the payload and run the DELETE or PUT operation.

We have used PUT, POST, DELETE and GET: the HTTP PUT was the Update, the HTTP POST was the Create, the HTTP DELETE was the Delete and the HTTP GET was the record selection.

Let us check the SAPUI5 application that has already been built for testing our scenarios.

The application has `sap.m.Input` boxes and three `sap.m.Buttons`.

Let us create a new record, with the first entry as `0000000011`, by pressing the Add button and checking if it gets created in the DB.

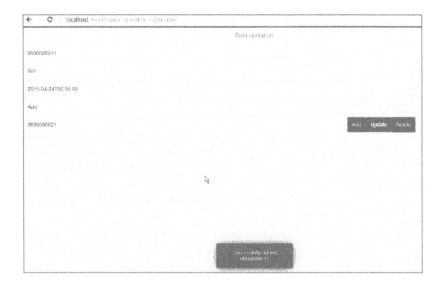

If we go to the table and refresh it, you will be able to see this newly created record.

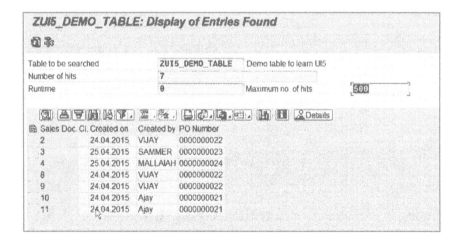

Let's go back to the browser and change the name of the record to 'Sammer' by pressing the Update button.
 If we go back and check the table again, we find that it has been updated.

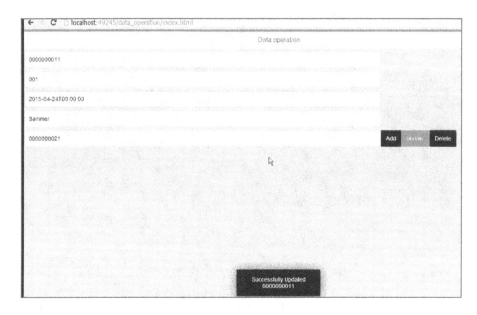

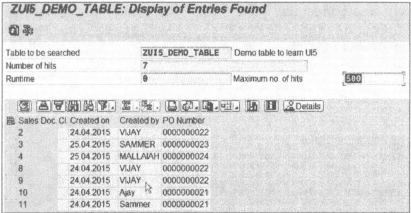

Finally, if we want to delete the record, we press the Delete button.

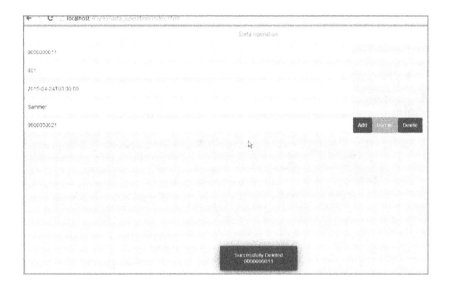

If the record is not present, then it is because it has been deleted.

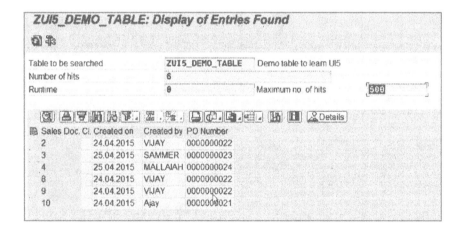

Let's see how these 3 features have been implemented. Let us go to Eclipse and create an SAPUI5 application.

The index page is simple.
index.html

```
<!DOCTYPEHTML>
<html><head>
<metahttp-equiv="X-UA-Compatible"content="IE=edge">
<metahttp-equiv='Content-
Type'content='text/html;charset=UTF-8'/>
<script src="resources/sap-ui-core.js"
id="sap-ui-bootstrap"
data-sap-ui-libs="sap.m"
data-sap-ui-theme="sap_bluecrystal">
</script>
<script>
sap.ui.localResources("data_operation");
var app = new sap.m.App({initialPage:"iddemoCalls1"});
var page = sap.ui.view({id:"iddemoCalls1",
viewName:"data_operation.demoCalls",
type:sap.ui.core.mvc.ViewType.JS});
app.addPage(page);
app.placeAt("content");
</script>
</head>
<bodyclass="sapUiBody"role="application">
<divid="content"></div>
</body>
</html>
```

We have by default one view page and one controller page.

demoCalls.view.js

```javascript
sap.ui.jsview("data_operation.demoCalls", {
/**
*Specifies the Controller belonging to this View. In
the case that it is
*not implemented, or that "null" is returned, this View
does not have a
*Controller.
*
*@memberOfdata_operation.demoCalls
*/
getControllerName : function() {
return"data_operation.demoCalls";
},
/**
*Is initially called once after the Controller has been
instantiated. It
*is the place where the UI is constructed. Since the
Controller is given
*to this method, its event handlers can be attached
right away.
*
*@memberOfdata_operation.demoCalls
*/
createContent : function(oController) {
return new sap.m.Page({
title : "Data operation",
content : [ new sap.m.Input("idZvblen", {
value : "0000000001",
width : "70%",
}), new sap.m.Input("idMandat", {
value : "001",
width : "70%",
}), new sap.m.Input("idZerdat", {
value : "2015-04-24T00:00:00",
width : "70%",
}), new sap.m.Input("idZernam", {
value : "Ajay",
width : "70%",
}), new sap.m.Input("idZbstnk", {
value : "0000000021",
width : "70%",
}), new sap.m.Button({
text : "Add",
type : sap.m.ButtonType.Accept,
```

```
press : [ "Add", oController.onSend,
oController ]
}), new sap.m.Button({
text : "Update",
type : sap.m.ButtonType.Emphasized,
press : [ "Update", oController.onSend,
oController ]
}), new sap.m.Button({
text : "Delete",
type : sap.m.ButtonType.Reject,
press : [ "Delete", oController.onSend,
oController ]
}) ]
});
}
});
```

In the view page, there are 5 inputs, `sap.m.Input`, and each one has an ID. These are the values that are displayed inside the input fields. We have given the width as 70% of the webpage.

There are also 3 buttons, `sap.m.Button`: Add, Update and Delete. The button type is to give the standard coloring of the buttons, for instance:

`type : sap.m.ButtonType.Emphasized,`

We have also the button press event like, `press : [ "Update", oController.onSend`.

If the button is pressed, it will call *onSend* method of controller with the parameter *"Update"*, for instance, which is the *sOperation* parameter of the *onSend* function, inside the controller page. The operation name values will be assigned to the *sOperation* and it will be passed during the *onSend* function call.

demoCalls.controller.js

```javascript
sap.ui.controller("data_operation.demoCalls",{
onInit :function() {
$.ajax({
type : "GET",
url :
"http://<DNS/IP>:8200/sap/opu/odata/sap/Z_DEMO_TEST4_SR
V/ZUI5_demo
_tableSet/?$format=json",
dataType : "json",
headers : {
"X-Requested-With" : "XMLHttpRequest",
"Content-Type" : "application/atom+xml",
"DataServiceVersion" : "2.0",
"X-CSRF-Token" : "Fetch"
},
success : function(data, response, xhr) {
sap.ui.getCore().setModel(xhr.getResponseHeader('x-
csrftoken'),
"csrftoken");
},
error : function(error) {
alert("Problem in connection");
console.log(error);
}
});
},
onSend :function(evt, sOperation) {
var oModel = new sap.ui.model.odata.ODataModel(
"http://<DNS/IP>/sap/opu/odata/sap/Z_DEMO_TEST4_SRV/")
var oData = {
Zvblen : sap.ui.getCore().byId("idZvblen")
.getValue(),
Zerdat : sap.ui.getCore().byId("idZerdat")
.getValue(),
Zernam : sap.ui.getCore().byId("idZernam")
.getValue(),
Zbstnk : sap.ui.getCore().byId("idZbstnk")
.getValue(),
};
if (sOperation === "Add") {
oModel.create('ZUI5_demo_tableSet',oData,null,
function() {
sap.m.MessageToast
.show('Successfully added '
```

```
+ oData.Zvblen);
},
function() {
sap.m.MessageToast
.show('Error in Adding new record');
});
} elseif (sOperation === "Update") {
oModel.update('ZUI5_demo_tableSet(\''+ oData.Zvblen +
'\')',
oData,
null,
function() {
sap.m.MessageToast
.show('Successfully Updated '
+ oData.Zvblen);
},
function() {
sap.m.MessageToast
.show('Error in Updating record');
});
} elseif (sOperation === "Delete") {
oModel.remove('ZUI5_demo_tableSet(\''
+ oData.Zvblen + '\')', null, function() {
sap.m.MessageToast.show('Successfully Deleted '
+ oData.Zvblen);
}, function() {
sap.m.MessageToast
.show('Error in Updating record');
});
} else {
}
}
});
```

In the controller, there is an AJAX call in *onInit* method that is called when the application is initialized ,with the main purpose of getting you authorized.

The AJAX call, which in this case is a GET to a specific service in order to read records, will ask us for username and password in a standard pop-up message.

Once we give the username and password, all the other calls from the same application will not require any more accesses as they will use the same credentials and authentication.

In this method, we also set the model for the header X-CSRF-Token in order to store it.

Next, in the `onSend` function, the specific operation passed in the parameter, which can be add, update or delete, will be executed.

We store all the values inside a JSON object named `oData` with keys ZVBLEN, ZERDAT, ZERNAM, and ZBSTK.

To get them, go to the Gateway Client and filter it with `$format=json`.

Execute and copy.

These are all the key fields that you need to use, keeping the lower/upper case.

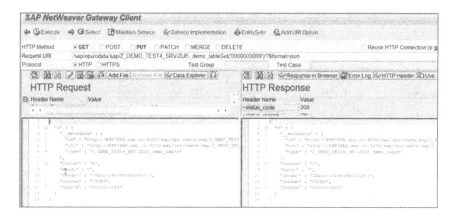

At the top of the `onSend` function, we can see the model object `oModel`.

This is the standard class reference that will use to get access to an object which has all capabilities to create, update and remove.

If we go to the browser, and open the SAPUI5 documentation, we can see the full class documentation of `sap.ui.model.odata.ODAtaModel`. We will use this class and the functions present inside this class.

Once we get the object *ODataModel*, we must pass the
following service name URL to it, in order to get access to all
operations like create, update, and remove or delete:
http://<DNS/IP>:<port>/sap/opu/odata/sap/Z_DEMO_T
EST4_SRV/
sOperation is the parameter of *onSend* function and is used
in order to trigger the specific operation like add, update or
delete and building the relevant URL we saw in the Gateway.
Let us go back to the Gateway client.

After the service URL, we pass a specific different string
depending on the operation. Operation is therefore the-first
parameter for *oModel*.

For instance:

```
oModel.create('ZUI5_demo_tableSet',oData,null,
```

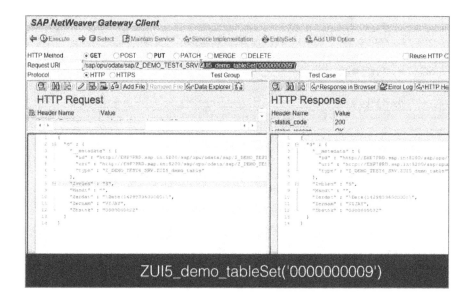

ZUI5_demo_tableSet('0000000009')

- When we create, we only pass Set.
- When we update, we pass Set and the value that should be updated.
- When we delete, we also pass the Set with the key parameter that should be removed.

The next parameter is the data that is required in the create and update processes.

For instance:

```
oModel.update('ZUI5_demo_tableSet(\''+
oData.Zvblen + '\')',
oData,
```

In the delete or remove processes, we don't t require data because it will delete the record based on the key we have provided.

After that, there is a null parameter, followed by two functions: if we have *functionSuccess*, then the first function is executed; if we have *functionFailure*, then the second function will be executed. This is the same throughout the create, update and remove processes.

For instance:

```
oModel.remove('ZUI5_demo_tableSet(\''
+ oData.Zvblen + '\')', null, function() {
sap.m.MessageToast.show('Successfully Deleted '
+ oData.Zvblen);
}, function() {
sap.m.MessageToast
.show('Error in Updating record');
});
```

sap.m. MessageToast is a small popup message that shows up for about 3 seconds.

The SAPUI5 application takes the filled values and, according to the button that is pressed, it will execute the specific function of the model.

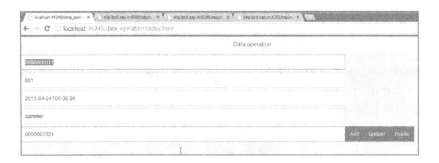

There are few things to remember here.

The first is that you should not start your Chrome browser directly from the Desktop, because you are doing a local development.

If you want to do an AJAX operation to a server from your local host, it won't be allowed in the Chrome.

You must open Chrome in a security-disabled mode by right-clicking on the Chrome icon, and selecting Properties, then copying the location of the Chrome application and changing the directory on cmd.exe.

Write this special command: *chrome.exe —disable-web-security*

Firefox will work fine without disabling the web security.

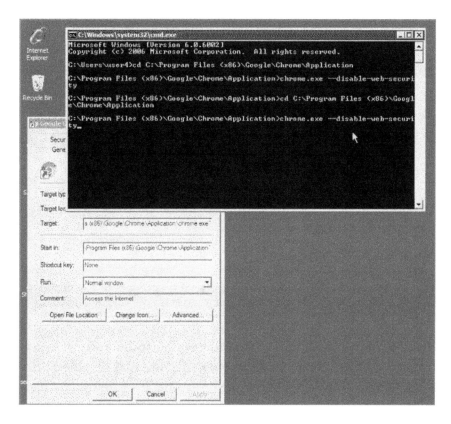

Let us open the Eclipse and copy the URL of the application that we see in the browser. This will call the *init ()* method, and its GET function, and will trigger the authorization check from SAP. Below we can see the standard SAP login where we must enter the username and password.

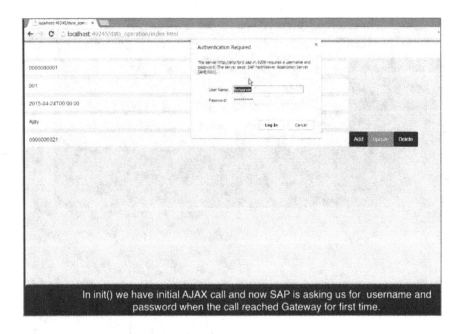

In init() we have initial AJAX call and now SAP is asking us for username and password when the call reached Gateway for first time.

The call we do in the *init ()* is to get the initial authorization. Once we are authorized by the backend, we will be able to do all the other operations like create, update, and delete, using *oModel: sap.ui.model.odata.ODataModel.*

Now that we got authorized, our files have the information of the authentication, so that next time when we do a call, it won't ask again, for this particular session.

In case we get errors during the tests, we should look at transaction */IWFND/ERROR_LOG* to see all errors that have occurred. By clicking on the time stamp we get all the details in the Error Context.

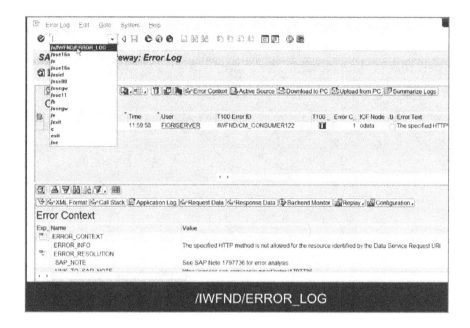

/IWFND/ERROR_LOG

The key of the table is `Zvblen`. You can see here that we have put a '\'. This is because when we want a new URL, we cannot write ' because it stands for end of the string in JavaScript. Therefore use escape sequence '\' in the beginning and in the end of the key parameter.

In the Chrome browser, if you go to Inspect Element and to the Network tab, and try to do an update, you will see that your URL looks like this:

```
http://<DNS/IP>:<port>/sap/opu/odata/sap/Z_DEMO_TEST4_S
RV/ZUI5_demo_table Set('0000000014')
```

If we try to delete this record, we pass the *oModel* for deleting this key. Once you have the entire app set up, you can also push this code to SAP.

Sharing SAPUI5 Project into SAP

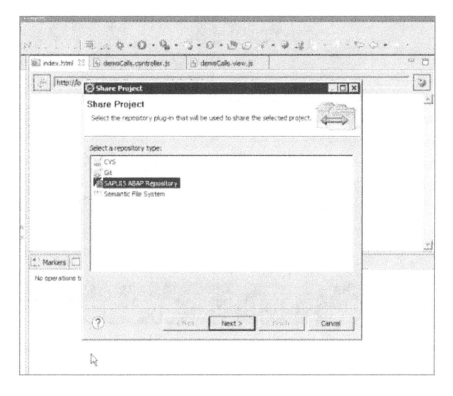

In Eclipse, right-click on data operation, go to Team and select Share Project. Select which SAP system where you want to push the SAPUI5 code.

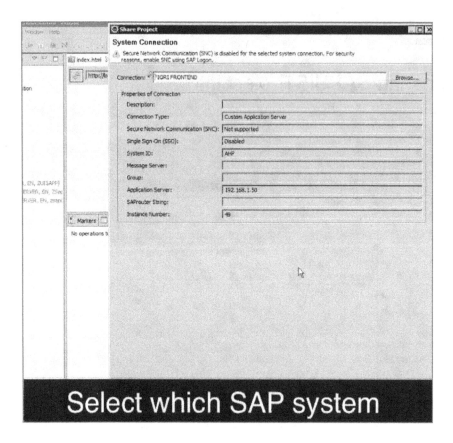

Select which SAP system

It will ask for the client, username and password for the SAP logon.

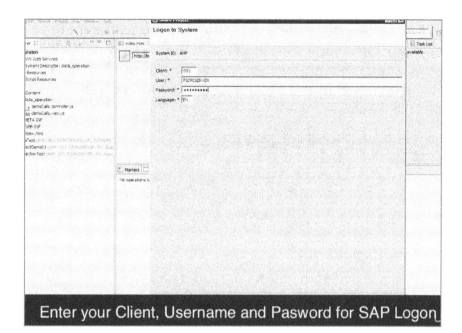

Enter your Client, Username and Pasword for SAP Logon

After that, select the BSP application.
If you have any BSP application, then you can filter it from
here, otherwise you can create a new one.

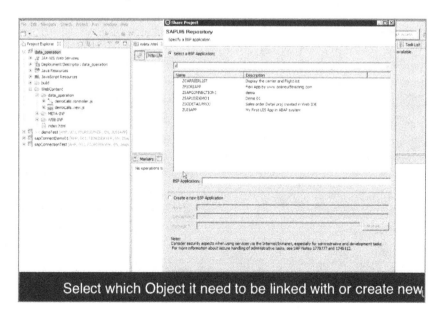

Select which Object it need to be linked with or create new

We will create a new BSP application for this demonstration. Let us give the name, description and the package. If you have any existing package, you can manually type it in, or you can filter as well. Let us use $TMP to make it a local object. After that click Finish.

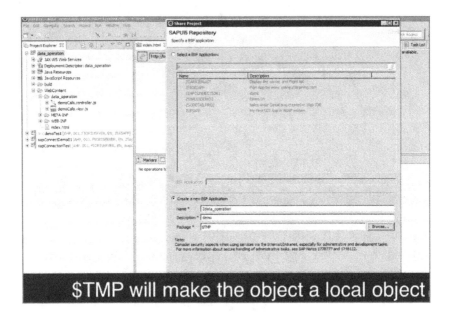

$TMP will make the object a local object

Now, we have successfully created this project inside our SAP.

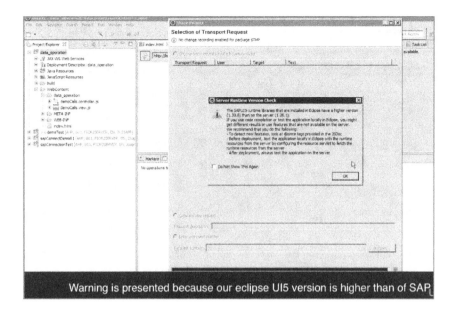

Warning is presented because our eclipse UI5 version is higher than of SAP

We will push our shared project. Right-click on data operation, go to Team and select Submit. Select all the files which will be shared to SAP, then click Finish.

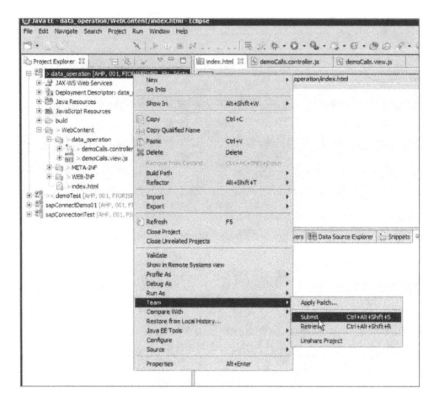

Go to the SE80 transaction and go inside the BSP application. Select the object name that we just pushed (ZDATA_OPERATION).

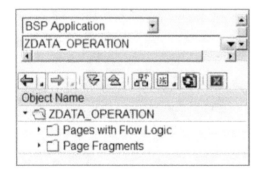

Let's run our application. Navigate to the index page and test it.

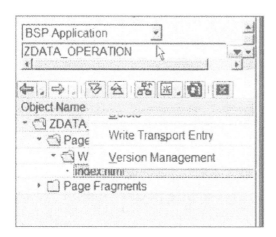

The default behavior opens the Internet Explorer.

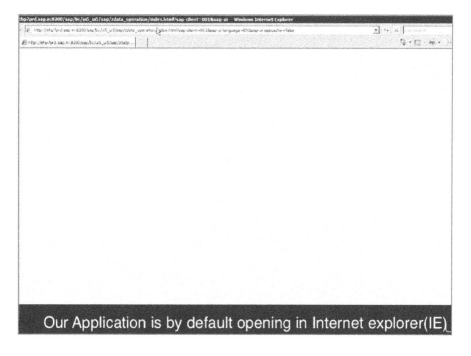

Our Application is by default opening in Internet explorer(IE)

You can see some of the fields, like client name, language and app caches, are appended to the end of the URL by default. If we copy the URL and paste in Chrome browser then we can see the application running.

Data operation

000000001

001

2015-04-24T00:00:00

Ajay

0000000021   Add   Update   Delete

Summary

We saw CRUDQ operations from SAPUI5 application and we came to know how the services we built in the previous section can be used by the frontend developer in the SAPUI5 applications.

As these services are exposed as REST-based services, or specifically OData protocol-based services, they can be utilized in many other applications.

If you are building an Android or a Java application, or even PHP applications, these services will be able to communicate and do the exact work of giving data and executing operations in your SAP backend.

We also saw how to push the SAPUI5 application to SAP, how to launch it from SAP into your browser and how to use it.

Chapter 5: Advanced Implementation of Services for Fiori and SAPUI5 Apps – SAP Gateway 2.0 Features

Some business objects, such as Sales Orders or Purchase Orders, consist of header and line item data. Thus, when creating such business objects, it makes sense to use hierarchical or nested data in the creation request. SAP Gateway can be used to create and expose a service that allows the creation of these business objects.

In SAP Gateway, the OData Channel provides deep insert functionality to accommodate the creation of an entity along with its associated entities in one request. The deep insert functionality is provided in ABAP interface /IWBEP/IF_MGW_APPL_SRV_RUNTIME, method CREATE_DEEP_ENTITY.

This chapter covers how to create and test an SAP Gateway service that can be used to QUERY, READ, and CREATE a Sales Order in an ECC system. However, the main focus is on the CREATE operation using the deep insert functionality, provided in the OData channel starting with SAP Gateway 2.0, SP2.

Before the creation of the service, it is important to analyze the BAPI and RFC that will be called and their parameters, in order to decide what type of HTTP operation one should use: POST or GET and what service method.

In case the function has tables as import parameters, either in Import or Table tab, the recommendation is going with an HTTP POST and the method CREATE_DEEP_ENTITY. Although this method is used to CREATE, depending on the complexity of RFC and BAPI parameters, it can be used to READ and QUERY.

In case the function has only a few variables or a small structure as import parameters we should use the HTTP GET and method /IWBEP/IF_MGW_APPL_SRV_RUNTIME ~ GET_EXPANDED_ENTITYSET. This method retrieves the BAPI results in a unique response and has the option to be customizable, where we can choose what kind of export parameter result, we want as the HTTP response.

So, in short:

CREATE_DEEP_ENTITY for CREATE or READ operations, if BAPI/RFC has complex import parameters.

GET_EXPANDED_ENTITYSET / GET_EXPANDED_ENTITY for CREATE or READ operations, if BAPI/RFC has simple import parameters.

CREATE_DEEP_ENTITY implementation

First, before the creation of our service, it's important to analyze the BAPI/RFC, its parameters and its specific functionality, like creation or reading.

Our example is the RFC YV_TRAIT_SALES_HISTORY_BC where we first start to check its parameters to understand if they are complex.

Below, we can see that in Import tab there are only simple variable parameters but in Table tab there are several parameter tables.

Based on this finding, the POST method with CREATE_DEEP_ENTITY service is the most suitable scenario since the payload will have all the input and will be more readable than passing complex and long parameters in a GET HTTP URL.

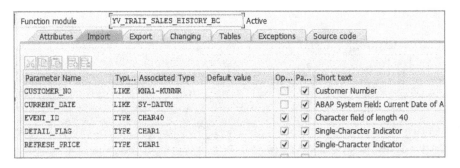

Function module: `YV_TRAIT_SALES_HISTORY_BC` — Active

Attributes | Import | Export | Changing | Tables | Exceptions | Source code

Parameter Name	Typi...	Associated Type	Default value	Op...	Pa...	Short text
CUSTOMER_NO	LIKE	KNA1-KUNNR		☐	✔	Customer Number
CURRENT_DATE	LIKE	SY-DATUM		☐	✔	ABAP System Field: Current Date of A
EVENT_ID	TYPE	CHAR40		✔	✔	Character field of length 40
DETAIL_FLAG	TYPE	CHAR1		✔	✔	Single-Character Indicator
REFRESH_PRICE	TYPE	CHAR1		✔	✔	Single-Character Indicator

Attributes | Import | Export | Changing | Tables | Exceptions | Source code

Parameter Name	Typing	Associated Type	Pass Val...	Short text
CUSTOMER_NO_OUT	LIKE	KNA1-KUNNR	✔	Customer Number
CURRENT_DATE_OUT	LIKE	SY-DATUM	✔	ABAP System Field: Current Date of A.
EVENT_ID_OUT	TYPE	CHAR40	✔	Character field of length 40

| Attributes | Import | Export | Changing | Tables | Exceptions | Source code |

Parameter Name	Typing	Associated Type	Optional	Short text
INPUT_DATA	LIKE	YVTRAIT_ROYALTY_INP..	☐	Trait Royalty Input Structure
OUTPUT_DATA	LIKE	YVTRAIT_ROYALTY_OUT..	☐	Trait Royalty Output Structure
DETAIL_DATA	LIKE	YVTRAIT_ROYALTY_OUT..	☐	Trait Royalty Output Structure in Det..
ERROR_DATA	LIKE	YBC_ERROR2	☑	Errors returned from Business Connec..
			☐	

Now that we have chosen POST and CREATE_DEEP_ENTITY method, let's start the creation of the service.

First, we create the entity types based on the RFC import parameters. Below there are the 5 entity types related to the RFC parameters:

- HistInput is the INPUT_DATA function table parameter
- HistOutput is the OUTPUT_DATA function table parameter
- HistDetail is the DETAIL_DATA function table parameter
- HistError is the ERROR_DATA function table parameter
- HistHeader is the entity that wraps all Import and Export single parameters

HistHeader will be the leading entity that defines the relationships with the other four entities.

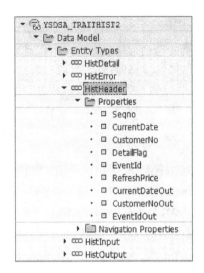

In order to create the entities and the respective entity sets, we will browse the RFC structures:

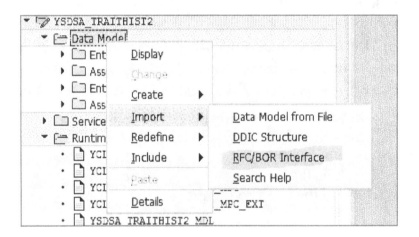

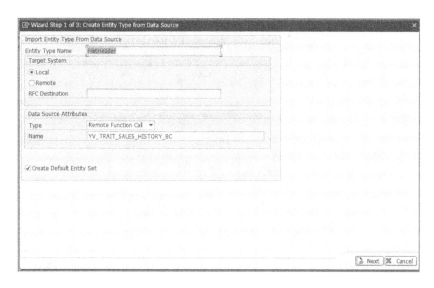

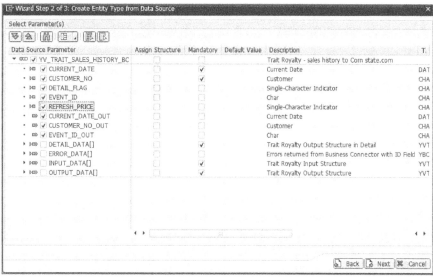

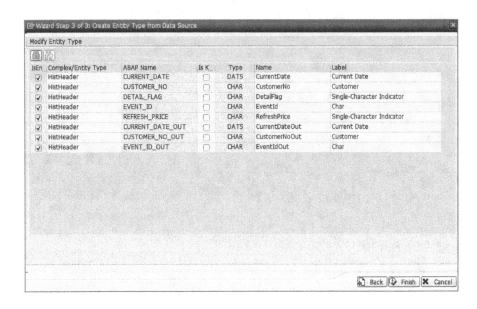

After pressing Finish, we add an additional field, Seqno, as the key field.

All entities need to be related in 1 to 1, N to M or 1 to N relation and usually the BAPIs/RFCs don't have this relationship clearly defined in their parameters.

For instance, a Sales Order creation BAPI has the header and items relation clearly defined but this is an exception in most RFCs. Therefore, we need to add another parameter, Seqno, to define the relationship.

Next, we repeat this same step for the remaining RFC interface parameters, and we get the below entities and their entity sets.

After having all entities and entity sets created, we define the relationships between them:

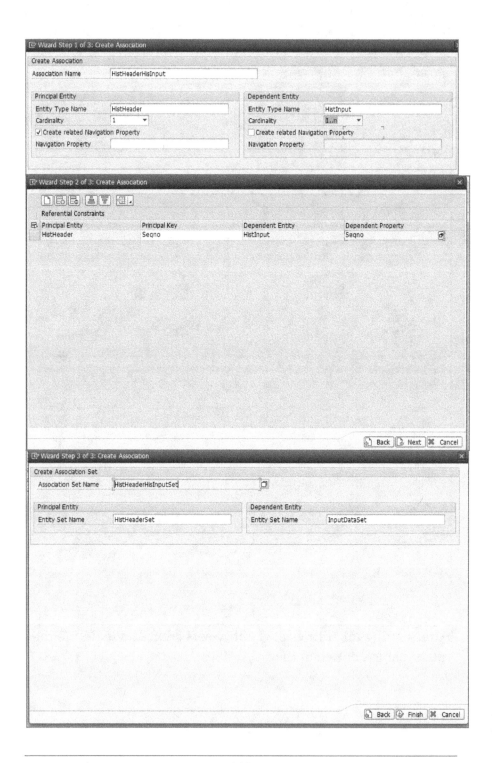

We repeat this step for the other 3 entities, and we get the below Associations and Association Sets.

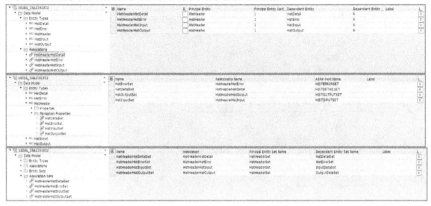

In short, HistHeader Entity has a relation 1:N with the other 4 entities.

From the design side, this is all. Now we will jump to the generation and coding of the provider class custom methods. Press generation button in order to generate the runtime artifacts.

Our 2 providers method classes are:
YCL_YSDSA_TRAITHIST2_DPC_EXT - Data Provider Extension Class.
YCL_YSDSA_TRAITHIST2_MPC_EXT- Model Provider Extension Class

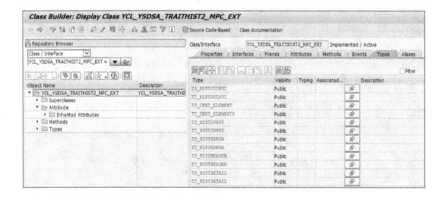

Double click in YCL_YSDSA_TRAITHIST2_MPC_EXT
Model Provider Class, in order to go to the ABAP workbench.
This class has all the data model variables, generated in ABAP
from the entity type properties defined in the SAP Gateway.

```abap
 8      types:
 9  ⊟    begin of TS_HISTOUTPUT,
10          SEQNO type C length 3,
11          YYMATNR type C length 18,
12          YYPLTYP type C length 2,
13          YYAUGRU type C length 3,
14          YYYEAR type C length 4,
15          YYNETPRICE type P length 9 decimals 3,
16          YYPERIOD_UNIT1 type P length 8 decimals 3,
17          YYPERIOD_UNIT2 type P length 8 decimals 3,
18          YYPERIOD_UNIT3 type P length 8 decimals 3,
19          YYPERIOD_UNIT4 type P length 8 decimals 3,
20      end of TS_HISTOUTPUT. .
21      types:
22    TT_HISTOUTPUT type standard table of TS_HISTOUTPUT.
33      types:
34  ⊟    begin of TS_HISTINPUT,
35          SEQNO type C length 3,
36          YYMATNR type C length 18,
37          YYPLTYP type C length 2,
38          YYAUGRU type C length 3,
39          YYPERIOD type C length 1,
40          YYYEAR type C length 4,
41          YYBUSINESS type C length 4,
42      end of TS_HISTINPUT. .
43      types:
44    TT_HISTINPUT type standard table of TS_HISTINPUT.
45      types:
46  ⊟    begin of TS_HISTERROR,
47          SEQNO type C length 3,
48          YYERROR type C length 6,
49          YYID type C length 20,
50          YYDESC type C length 132,
51      end of TS_HISTERROR. .
52      types:
53    TT_HISTERROR type standard table of TS_HISTERROR.
```

```
54    types:
55  ⊟  begin of TS_HISTHEADER,
56  │      SEQNO type C length 3,
57  │      CURRENTDATE type C length 8,
58  │      CUSTOMER_NO type C length 10,
59  │      DETAIL_FLAG type C length 1,
60  │      EVENT_ID type C length 40,
61  │      REFRESH_PRICE type C length 1,
62  │      CURRENTDATEOUT type string,
63  │      CUSTOMER_NO_OUT type C length 10,
64  │      EVENT_ID_OUT type C length 40,
65  └    end of TS_HISTHEADER. .
66    types:
67   TT_HISTHEADER type standard table of TS_HISTHEADER.
68    types:
69  ⊟  begin of TS_HISTDETAIL,
70  │      SEQNO type C length 3,
71  │      YYMATNR type C length 18,
72  │      YYPLTYP type C length 2,
73  │      YYAUGRU type C length 3,
74  │      YYYEAR type C length 4,
75  │      YYNETPRICE type P length 9 decimals 3,
76  │      YYQUANTITY type P length 7 decimals 3,
77  │      YYNETWR type P length 9 decimals 3,
78  │      YYPRICEDATE type C length 8,
79  │      YYDOCDATE type C length 8,
80  │      YYDOCTYPE type C length 4,
81  │      YYDOCNUM type C length 10,
82  │      YYPURORD type C length 17,
83  └    end of TS_HISTDETAIL. .
84    types:│
85   TT_HISTDETAIL type standard table of TS_HISTDETAIL.
```

Before starting to develop the solution in the Data Provider Class YCL_YSDSA_TRAITHIST2_DPC_EXT always double check first that the generated ABAP data types in the MPC_EXT are what you expect, based on what you have designed in SAP GW, in the entity type properties.
In class YCL_YSDSA_TRAITHIST2_DPC_EXT, we need first to redefine method CREATE_DEEP_ENTITY.

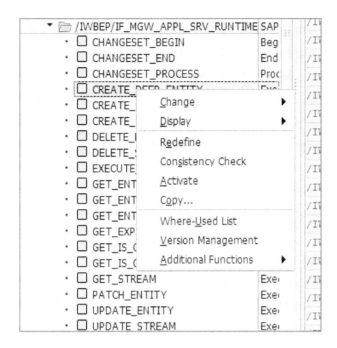

After the redefinition, it is critical to define the data type following always the very same naming that has been defined for the entities in the SAP GW side. This is a major important detail that will save a lot of time in error troubleshooting.

Type `ty_str_exp` contains 4 internal tables that need to be <u>exactly</u> `histinputset`, `histoutputset`, `hustdetailset` and `histerrorset`, since these are the names of the SAP GW entities. In relation to the header structure, we need simply to include the type defined in the Model Class. As we can see below, we should use the generated types of the Model Class as the code will be cleaner and less error prone because we are referring directly to the model class structure with
`ycl_ysdsa_traithist2_mpc_ext=>ts_histinput=>`.

The Header entity is the leading entity thas has 1:N relationship with the other 4 entities through the *Seqno* field, therefore it is this entityset that will be used to start the process, by reading the entire payload input data with `io_data_provider->read_entry_data( IMPORTING es_data = lw_deep )`

As soon as we get the HistHeaderSet entityset, we read the entire input data into *lw_deep* variable, of type *ty_str_exp*.

```
29 ⊟      CASE lv_entityset_name.
30 ◊        WHEN 'HistHeaderSet'.
31            io_data_provider->read_entry_data( IMPORTING es_data = lw_deep ).
32
33            lv_kunnr          = lw_deep-customer_no.
34            lv_date           = lw_deep-currentdate.
35            lv_event          = lw_deep-event_id.
36            lv_detail_flag    = lw_deep-detail_flag.
37            lv_refresh_price  = lw_deep-refresh_price.
38
39 ⊟          LOOP AT lw_deep-histinputset ASSIGNING FIELD-SYMBOL(<ls_histinputset>).
40              APPEND INITIAL LINE TO lt_idata ASSIGNING FIELD-SYMBOL(<ls_idata>).
41              MOVE-CORRESPONDING <ls_histinputset> TO <ls_idata>.
42            ENDLOOP.
```

After this first reading step, it is important to declare separate variables that match the RFC/BAPI parameters. This way we will avoid short dumps with potential type mismatches between our *lw_deep* structure and the RFC parameter types.

As we see in the picture above, in the data declaration, we have the variables declared: *lt_idata, lt_odata, lt_detail, lt_error, lv_kunnr*, etc.
Before calling RFC YV_TRAIT_SALES_HISTORY_BC, all variables should be mapped beforehand as we can see.

```
44  *---------------------------------------------------------------
45  *  Call function module YV_TRAIT_SALES_HISTORY_BC
46  *---------------------------------------------------------------
47          CALL FUNCTION 'YV_TRAIT_SALES_HISTORY_BC'
48            EXPORTING
49              customer_no        = lv_kunnr
50              current_date       = lv_date
51              event_id           = lv_event
52              detail_flag        = lv_detail_flag
53              refresh_price      = lv_refresh_price
54            IMPORTING
55              customer_no_out    = lw_deep-customer_no_out
56              current_date_out   = lv_date_out
57              event_id_out       = lw_deep-event_id_out
58            TABLES
59              input_data         = lt_idata
60              output_data        = lt_odata
61              detail_data        = lt_detail
62              error_data         = lt_error.
63
```

RFC is called and we get the return in 4 output internal tables and in the 3 fields of the header, that correspond to the output.
The following step, depicted below, is wrapping the RFC return into *lw_deep* Model Class generated structure.

```abap
64    *---------------------------------------------------------
65    * Map the response to the caller interface
66    *---------------------------------------------------------
67          CLEAR lw_deep-histoutputset[].
68          LOOP AT lt_odata ASSIGNING FIELD-SYMBOL(<ls_odata>).
69            APPEND INITIAL LINE TO lw_deep-histoutputset ASSIGNING FIELD-SYMBOL(<ls_histoutputset>).
70            MOVE-CORRESPONDING <ls_odata> TO <ls_histoutputset>.
71          ENDLOOP.
72
73          CLEAR lw_deep-histdetailset[].
74          LOOP AT lt_detail ASSIGNING FIELD-SYMBOL(<ls_detail>).
75            APPEND INITIAL LINE TO lw_deep-histdetailset ASSIGNING FIELD-SYMBOL(<ls_histdetailset>).
76            MOVE-CORRESPONDING <ls_detail> TO <ls_histdetailset>.
77          ENDLOOP.
78
79          CLEAR lw_deep-histerrorset[].
80          LOOP AT lt_error ASSIGNING FIELD-SYMBOL(<ls_error>).
81            APPEND INITIAL LINE TO lw_deep-histerrorset ASSIGNING FIELD-SYMBOL(<ls_histerrorset>).
82            MOVE-CORRESPONDING <ls_error> TO <ls_histerrorset>.
83          ENDLOOP.
84
85          lw_deep-currentdateout = lv_date_out.
86
87          copy_data_to_ref( EXPORTING is_data = lw_deep
88                            CHANGING cr_data = er_deep_entity ).
89
90      ENDCASE.
91
92    ENDMETHOD.
```

In the end, it is very important to update the HTTP response, which is represented by *er_deep_entity*, by copying back the *lw_deep* RFC return values.

To test the service, you create the payload with exactly the same structure of type *ty_str_exp*.

Repository Browser

Class / Interface
YCL_YSDSA_TRAITHIST2_DPC_EXT ×

Object Name	Descr...
YCL_YSDSA_TRAITHIST2_DPC_EXT	Data Prov
▸ ▭ Superclasses	
▸ ▭ Attribute	
▾ ▭ Methods	
▸ ▭ Inherited Methods	
▾ ▭ Redefinitions	
▪ /IWBEP/IF_MGW_APPL_SRV_ Execute 2	
▸ ▭ Types	

```
METHOD /iwbep/if_mgw_appl_srv_runtime~create_deep_entity.

  TYPES: BEGIN OF ty_str_exp.
           INCLUDE       TYPE ycl_ysdsa_traithist2_mpc_ext~ts_histheader.
  TYPES: histinputset  TYPE STANDARD TABLE OF ycl_ysdsa_traithist2_mpc_ext~ts_histinput WITH EMPTY KEY.
  TYPES: histoutputset TYPE STANDARD TABLE OF ycl_ysdsa_traithist2_mpc_ext~ts_histoutput WITH EMPTY KEY.
  TYPES: histdetailset TYPE STANDARD TABLE OF ycl_ysdsa_traithist2_mpc_ext~ts_histdetail WITH EMPTY KEY.
  TYPES: histerrorset  TYPE STANDARD TABLE OF ycl_ysdsa_traithist2_mpc_ext~ts_histerror WITH EMPTY KEY.
  TYPES: END OF ty_str_exp.

*----------------------------------------------------------
* Data Declaration
*----------------------------------------------------------
  DATA: lt_idata          TYPE TABLE OF yvtrait_royalty_input,
        lt_odata          TYPE TABLE OF yvtrait_royalty_output,
        lt_detail         TYPE TABLE OF yvtrait_royalty_out_detail,
        lt_error          TYPE TABLE OF ybc_error2,
        lw_deep           TYPE ty_str_exp,
        lv_entityset_name TYPE string,
        lv_kunnr          TYPE kunnr,
        lv_date           TYPE sydatum,
        lv_event          TYPE char40,
        lv_detail_flag    TYPE char1,
        lv_refresh_price  TYPE char1,
        lv_date_out       TYPE sydatum.

  lv_entityset_name = io_tech_request_context->get_entity_set_name( ).
```

GET_EXPANDED_ENTITYSET

implementation

Before the creation of the service, it is important to analyze the BAPI and RFC that will be called and their parameters in order to decide what type of HTTP operation we should use: POST or GET and what service method.

As we have seen before, in the case our BAPI/RFC does not have complex import parameters we can choose an HTTP GET instead of a POST and passing the parameters in the URL.

Thus, in this scenario, we have another useful method /IWBEP/IF_MGW_APPL_SRV_RUNTIME ~ GET_EXPANDED_ENTITYSET / GET_EXPANDED_ENTITY that allows to return any complex BAPI export parameters and having the option to define, in the HTTP GET URL, what return we want to expand back in the HTTP response.

Our example is the RFC YSDSA_HAULBACK_DATAREQUEST where we first start to check its parameters to understand if they are complex.

Below, we can see that in Import tab there are only simple variable parameters but in Table tab there are complex tables that can be returned.

Based on this finding, the GET method with GET_EXPANDED_ENTITYSET service is the most suitable scenario since the import parameters are simple and few.

You could also go with a HTTP POST and CREATE_DEEP_ENTITY in this case.

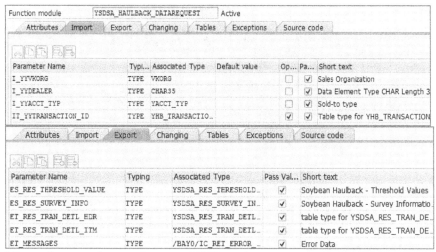

Function module	YSDSA_HAULBACK_DATAREQUEST	Active

| Attributes | Import | Export | Changing | Tables | Exceptions | Source code |

Parameter Name	Typl...	Associated Type	Default value	Op...	Pa...	Short text
I_YYVKORG	TYPE	VKORG		☐	☑	Sales Organization
I_YYDEALER	TYPE	CHAR35		☐	☑	Data Element Type CHAR Length 3
I_YYACCT_TYP	TYPE	YACCT_TYP		☐	☑	Sold-to type
IT_YYTRANSACTION_ID	TYPE	YHB_TRANSACTIO...		☑	☑	Table type for YHB_TRANSACTION

| Attributes | Import | Export | Changing | Tables | Exceptions | Source code |

Parameter Name	Typing	Associated Type	Pass Val...	Short text
ES_RES_THRESHOLD_VALUE	TYPE	YSDSA_RES_THRESHOLD...	☑	Soybean Haulback - Threshold Values
ES_RES_SURVEY_INFO	TYPE	YSDSA_RES_SURVEY_IN...	☑	Soybean Haulback - Survey Informatio.
ET_RES_TRAN_DETL_HDR	TYPE	YSDSA_RES_TRAN_DETL...	☑	table type for YSDSA_RES_TRAN_DE...
ET_RES_TRAN_DETL_ITM	TYPE	YSDSA_RES_TRAN_DETL...	☑	table type for YSDSA_RES_TRAN_DE...
ET_MESSAGES	TYPE	/BAYO/IC_RET_ERROR_...	☑	Error Data

Now that we have chosen GET and GET_EXPANDED_ENTITYSET method, let's start the creation of the service.

First, we create the entity types based on the RFC import parameters.

Below there are the 5 entity types related to the RFC parameters:

- HaulbackDetailHeader is the ET_RES_TRAN_DETL_HDR function table parameter
- HaulbackDetailItem is the ET_RES_TRAN_DETL_ITM function table parameter
- HaulbackError is the DE ET_MESSAGES function table parameter
- HaulbackHeader is the entity that wraps all Import single parameters
- HaulbackSurvey is the ES_RES_SURVEY_INFO function structure parameter
- HaulbackThreshold is the ES_RES_THRESHOLD_VALUE function structure parameter

HaulbackHeader will be the leading entity that defines the relationships with the other five entities through field Seqno.

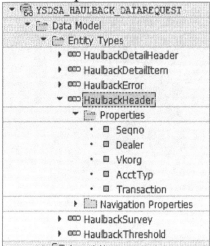

In order to create the entities and the respective entity sets, browse the RFC structures like explained in the previous section for the CREATE_DEEP_ENTITY scenario.

After pressing Finish, add an additional field, *Seqno*, as the key field, since all entities need to be related in 1 to 1, N to M or 1 to N relation and usually the BAPIs/RFCs don't have this relation clearly defined in their parameters.

Next, we repeat this same step for the remaining RFC interface parameters, and we get the below entities and their entity sets.

After having all entities and entity sets created, we define the relationships between them.

The five entities that are related to HaulbackHeader, 3 of them are tables and 2 are structures therefore, there will be 3 relations 1:N and 2 relations 1:1.

- HaulbackDetailHeader is a table
- HaulbackDetailItem is a table
- HaulbackError is a table
- HaulbackSurvey is a structure
- HaulbackThreshold is a structure
-

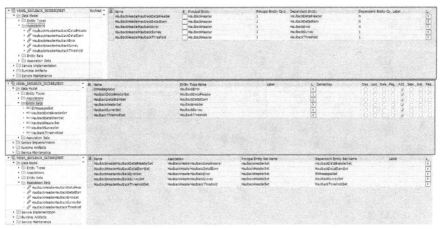

In short, HaulbackHeader Entity has a relation 1:N with HaulbackDetailHeader, HaulbackDetailItem and HaulbackError; and it has a relation 1:1 with HaulbackSurvey and HaulbackThreshold entities.

From the design side, this is all. Now we will jump to the generation and coding of the provider class custom methods. Press generation button in order to generate the runtime artifacts.

Our 2 providers method classes are:
YCL_YSDSA_HAULBACK_DAT_DPC_EXT - Data Provider
Extension Class.
YCL_YSDSA_HAULBACK_DAT_MPC_EXT - Model
Provider Extension Class

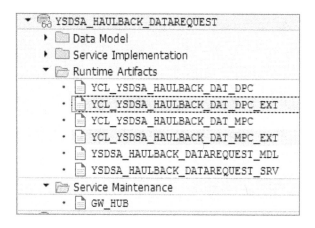

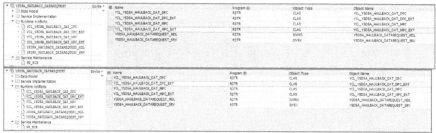

Double click in YCL_YSDSA_HAULBACK_DAT_MPC_EXT
Model Provider Class, in order to go to the ABAP workbench.
This class has all the data model variables generated in ABAP
from the entity type properties defined in the SAP Gateway.

```abap
TYPES:
  BEGIN OF ts_haulbackheader,
    seqno       TYPE c LENGTH 3,
    dealer      TYPE char35,
    vkorg       TYPE vkorg,
    acct_typ    TYPE c LENGTH 10,
    transaction TYPE string,
  END OF ts_haulbackheader.
TYPES:
tt_haulbackheader TYPE STANDARD TABLE OF ts_haulbackheader.
```

```abap
TYPES:
  BEGIN OF ts_haulbacksurvey,
    seqno          TYPE c LENGTH 3,
    yysbreturns    TYPE ylmon_sbreturns,
    yymulti_sh     TYPE ymulti_sh,
    yyhb_qty       TYPE ylmon_hb_qty,
    yybulkreturn   TYPE ybulkreturn,
    yysurvey_taken TYPE char1,
  END OF ts_haulbacksurvey.
TYPES:
tt_haulbacksurvey TYPE STANDARD TABLE OF ts_haulbacksurvey.
```

```
TYPES:
  BEGIN OF ts_haulbackdetailheader,
    seqno               TYPE c LENGTH 3,
    yytransaction_id    TYPE c LENGTH 20,
    yyship_to           TYPE c LENGTH 30,
    yyacct_typ          TYPE c LENGTH 10,
    yyname1             TYPE c LENGTH 35,
    yystras             TYPE c LENGTH 35,
    yyort01             TYPE c LENGTH 35,
    yyregio             TYPE c LENGTH 3,
    yypstlz             TYPE c LENGTH 10,
    yytelf1             TYPE c LENGTH 16,
    yypurchase_order    TYPE c LENGTH 20,
    yytotal_qty_ret     TYPE p LENGTH 7 DECIMALS 3,
    yytotal_est_cr      TYPE p LENGTH 9 DECIMALS 3,
    yytotal_est_db      TYPE p LENGTH 9 DECIMALS 3,
    yytot_est_net_cr    TYPE p LENGTH 9 DECIMALS 3,
    yystatus            TYPE c LENGTH 1,
    yystatus_desc       TYPE c LENGTH 35,
    yydcithreshold      TYPE p LENGTH 7 DECIMALS 3,
    yyhold_dci_thres    TYPE flag,
    yyhold_cr_thres     TYPE flag,
    yyorder_number      TYPE c LENGTH 10,
    yyinvoice_number    TYPE c LENGTH 10,
    yysubmit_date       TYPE timestampl,
    yysubmit_time       TYPE t,
    yycreate_date       TYPE timestampl,
    yycreate_time       TYPE t,
    yyupdate_date |     TYPE timestampl,
    yyupdate_time       TYPE t,
    yycreatedby         TYPE c LENGTH 65,
    yyupdatedby         TYPE c LENGTH 65,
    yysubmittedby       TYPE c LENGTH 65,
  END OF ts_haulbackdetailheader.
TYPES:
tt_haulbackdetailheader TYPE STANDARD TABLE OF ts_haulbackdetailheader.
```

```
TYPES:
  BEGIN OF ts_haulbackdetailitem,
    seqno              TYPE c LENGTH 3,
    yytransaction_id   TYPE c LENGTH 20,
    yyitem_no          TYPE c LENGTH 6,
    yymaterial         TYPE c LENGTH 18,
    yymat_typ          TYPE c LENGTH 10,
    yyupc_code         TYPE c LENGTH 18,
    yymat_typ2         TYPE c LENGTH 10,
    yygtin             TYPE c LENGTH 18,
    yymat_typ3         TYPE c LENGTH 10,
    yymaterial_descr   TYPE c LENGTH 40,
    yysales_unit       TYPE c LENGTH 3,
    yyorder_unit       TYPE p LENGTH 8 DECIMALS 3,
    yyseed_lb          TYPE c LENGTH 10,
    yybatch            TYPE c LENGTH 10,
    yynet_delivered    TYPE p LENGTH 7 DECIMALS 3,
    yyprevious_submi   TYPE p LENGTH 7 DECIMALS 3,
    yyqty_return       TYPE p LENGTH 7 DECIMALS 3,
    yyelevator_dump    TYPE timestampl,
    yycommodity_pric   TYPE p LENGTH 9 DECIMALS 3,
    yyest_credit       TYPE p LENGTH 9 DECIMALS 3,
    yyest_debit        TYPE p LENGTH 9 DECIMALS 3,
    yyest_net_credit   TYPE p LENGTH 9 DECIMALS 3,
    yyhb_price         TYPE p LENGTH 9 DECIMALS 3,
    yypricecuky        TYPE c LENGTH 5,
    yyhold_search_ba   TYPE flag,
  END OF ts_haulbackdetailitem.
TYPES:
tt_haulbackdetailitem TYPE STANDARD TABLE OF ts_haulbackdetailitem.
```

```
TYPES:
  BEGIN OF ts_haulbackerror,
    seqno        TYPE c LENGTH 3,
    msg_type     TYPE c LENGTH 1,
    msg_no       TYPE c LENGTH 3,
    msg_id       TYPE c LENGTH 20,
    msg_object   TYPE c LENGTH 50,
    msg_desc_int TYPE c LENGTH 200,
    msg_desc_ext TYPE c LENGTH 300,
  END OF ts_haulbackerror.
TYPES:
tt_haulbackerror TYPE STANDARD TABLE OF ts_haulbackerror.
```

Before starting to develop the solution in the Data Provider
Class YCL_YSDSA_HAULBACK_DAT_DPC_EXT always
double check first that the generated ABAP data types in the
MPC_EXT are what you expect, based on what you have
designed in SAP GW, in the entity type properties.

In class YCL_YSDSA_HAULBACK_DAT_DPC_EXT, we need
first to redefine the 3 needed methods:

YCL_YSDSA_HAULBACK_DAT_DPC_EXT	Data Provider Secondary Class
▸ ☐ Superclasses	
▸ ☐ Attribute	
▾ ☐ Methods	
▸ ☐ Inherited Methods	
▾ ☐ Redefinitions	
· ☐ /IWBEP/IF_MGW_APPL_SRV_RUNTIME~GET_EXPANDED_ENTITY	Execute a READ request (CReadUD) - ENTRY with inlines -
· ☐ /IWBEP/IF_MGW_APPL_SRV_RUNTIME~GET_EXPANDED_ENTITYSET	Execute a READ request (CReadUD) - ENTRY with inlines -
· △ HAULBACKHEADERSE_GET_ENTITYSET	Related EntitySet Name: HaulbackHeaderSet
▸ ☐ Types	

- **HAULBACKHEADERSE_GET_ENTITYSET** – starting point call from HTTP GET
- **/IWBEP/IF_MGW_APPL_SRV_RUNTIME~GET_EX PANDED_ENTITYSET**, for the export table parameters
- **/IWBEP/IF_MGW_APPL_SRV_RUNTIME~GET_EX PANDED_ENTITY**, for the export structure parameters

Since we will use the HTTP GET, the first method to be called, the starting point, is the HAULBACKHEADERSE_GET_ENTITYSET.

Therefore, in this method, we will read the HTTP GET URL parameters.

```
METHOD haulbackheaderse_get_entityset.
  DATA: ls_header        TYPE ycl_ysdsa_haulback_dat_mpc_ext=>ts_haulbackheader,
        ls_threshold     TYPE ysdsa_res_threshold_values,
        ls_survey        TYPE ysdsa_res_survey_info,
        lt_details_header TYPE ysdsa_res_tran_detl_hdr_tab,
        lt_details_item  TYPE ysdsa_res_tran_detl_itm_tab,
        lt_message       TYPE /bay0/ic_ret_error_tab,
        lt_transaction   TYPE yhb_transaction_id_tab.

  "Get filter object from request
  DATA(lo_filter) = io_tech_request_context->get_filter( ).
  DATA(lt_filters) = lo_filter->get_filter_select_options( ).

  "Read filter URL data
  LOOP AT lt_filters INTO DATA(ls_filters).
    DATA(ls_select_options) = VALUE #( ls_filters-select_options[ 1 ] OPTIONAL ).
    CASE ls_filters-property.
      WHEN 'SEQNO'.
        ls_header-seqno = ls_select_options-low.
      WHEN 'DEALER'.
        ls_header-dealer = |{ ls_select_options-low ALPHA = IN }|.
      WHEN 'VKORG'.
        ls_header-vkorg = ls_select_options-low.
      WHEN 'ACCT_TYP'.
        ls_header-acct_typ = ls_select_options-low.
      WHEN 'TRANSACTION'.
        LOOP AT ls_filters-select_options INTO ls_select_options.
          APPEND INITIAL LINE TO lt_transaction ASSIGNING FIELD-SYMBOL(<ls_transaction>).
          <ls_transaction> = ls_select_options-low.
        ENDLOOP.
    ENDCASE.
  ENDLOOP.
```

From the request call, we first get the GET parameters, or select options, into our local internal table, through:

```
DATA(lt_filters) = lo_filter-
>get_filter_select_options( ).
```
Afterwards, we check each of them and move to a local header structure
```
ls_header            TYPE
ycl_ysdsa_haulback_dat_mpc_ext=>ts_haulbackheader,
```
The *TRANSACTION* import parameter is a table but not complex so it is ok to pass it into the URL although you can see there is an additional processing to read it:
```
     LOOP AT ls_filters-select_options INTO
ls_select_options.
         APPEND INITIAL LINE TO lt_transaction
ASSIGNING FIELD-SYMBOL(<ls_transaction>).
         <ls_transaction> = ls_select_options-low.
     ENDLOOP.
```
Afterwards we call the BAPI/RFC and get the return into our local tables and structures:
```
"Call local function
 CALL FUNCTION 'YSDSA_HAULBACK_DATAREQUEST'
   EXPORTING
     i_yyvkorg   |          = ls_header-vkorg
     i_yydealer             = ls_header-dealer
     i_yyacct_typ           = ls_header-acct_typ
     it_yytransaction_id    = lt_transaction
   IMPORTING
     es_res_threshold_value = ls_threshold
     es_res_survey_info     = ls_survey
     et_res_tran_detl_hdr   = lt_details_header
     et_res_tran_detl_itm   = lt_details_item
     et_messages            = lt_message.
```
Finally, we move the return into class internal attributes in order they can be used in the other 2 methods:
GET_EXPANDED_ENTITYSET and
GET_EXPANDED_ENTITY

```
"Bundle return data
LOOP AT lt_details_header ASSIGNING FIELD-SYMBOL(<ls_details_header>).
  APPEND INITIAL LINE TO gt_haulback_detail_header ASSIGNING FIELD-SYMBOL(<ls_haulback_detail_header>).
  MOVE-CORRESPONDING <ls_details_header> TO <ls_haulback_detail_header>.
ENDLOOP.

LOOP AT lt_details_item ASSIGNING FIELD-SYMBOL(<ls_details_item>).
  APPEND INITIAL LINE TO gt_haulback_detail_item ASSIGNING FIELD-SYMBOL(<ls_haulback_detail_item>).
  MOVE-CORRESPONDING <ls_details_item> TO <ls_haulback_detail_item>.
ENDLOOP.

LOOP AT lt_message ASSIGNING FIELD-SYMBOL(<ls_message>).
  APPEND INITIAL LINE TO gt_haulback_error ASSIGNING FIELD-SYMBOL(<ls_haulback_error>).
  MOVE-CORRESPONDING <ls_message> TO <ls_haulback_error>.
ENDLOOP.

MOVE-CORRESPONDING: ls_threshold TO gs_haulback_threshold,
                    ls_survey    TO gs_haulback_survey.

APPEND INITIAL LINE TO et_entityset ASSIGNING FIELD-SYMBOL(<fs_entityset>).
MOVE-CORRESPONDING ls_header TO <fs_entityset>.
<fs_entityset>-seqno = ls_header-seqno.
```

These 2 methods are called after the call of HAULBACKHEADERSE_GET_ENTITYSET has been finished.

After the first method has been finished, let's start the GET_EXPANDED_ENTITY.

```
Method    /IWBEP/IF_MGW_APPL_SRV_RUNTIME~GET_EXPANDED_ENTITY          Active

 1  ⊟  METHOD /iwbep/if_mgw_appl_srv_runtime~get_expanded_entity.
 2
 3  ⊟    CASE iv_entity_name.
 4         WHEN 'HaulbackDetailHeader'.
 5  ⊟      TRY.
 6           CALL METHOD super->/iwbep/if_mgw_appl_srv_runtime~get_expanded_entity
 7             EXPORTING
 8               iv_entity_name          = iv_entity_name
 9               iv_entity_set_name      = iv_entity_set_name
10               iv_source_name          = iv_source_name
11               it_key_tab              = it_key_tab
12               it_navigation_path      = it_navigation_path
13               io_expand               = io_expand
14               io_tech_request_context = io_tech_request_context
15             IMPORTING
16               er_entity               = er_entity
17               es_response_context     = es_response_context
18               et_expanded_clauses     = et_expanded_clauses
19               et_expanded_tech_clauses = et_expanded_tech_clauses.
20
21           CATCH /iwbep/cx_mgw_busi_exception .
22           CATCH /iwbep/cx_mgw_tech_exception .
23         ENDTRY.
24
25       WHEN 'HaulbackSurvey'.
26         copy_data_to_ref(
27           EXPORTING
28             is_data = gs_haulback_survey
29           CHANGING
30             cr_data = er_entity ).
31
32       WHEN 'HaulbackThreshold'.
33         copy_data_to_ref(
34           EXPORTING
35             is_data = gs_haulback_threshold
36           CHANGING
37             cr_data = er_entity ).
38     ENDCASE.
39
40  ENDMETHOD.
```

This method will move back the global structure variables, not
tables, to the HTTP response in case we mention them in
HTTP GET URL with the expand option. These entities that
are retuned back are the ones that have a 1:1 relationship with
the header.

In case we need to get the return of these structures, we
simply call the following URL from Gateway Client:

```
/sap/opu/odata/SAP/YSDSA_HAULBACK_DATAREQUEST_SRV/Haulb
ackHeaderSet?$expand=HaulbackSurvey,HaulbackThreshold
```

As we can see above, the starting point is the
HaulbackHeaderSet and therefore the URL needs to start
with:

```
/sap/opu/odata/SAP/YSDSA_HAULBACK_DATAREQUEST_SRV/Haulb
ackHeaderSet
```

In front of the main part of the URL, we pass the GET
parameters

```
?$filter=Kunnr eq '4999' and Eventid eq  'CSSN' and
Date eq  '20190130' and ProdPltyp eq 'MATNR'
```
or options like the expand option:
```
?$expand=HaulbackSurvey,HaulbackThreshold
```
Finally, let's develop the GET_EXPANDED_ENTITYSET.

Method	/IWBEP/IF_MGW_APPL_SRV_RUNTIME~GET_EXPANDED_ENTITYSET	Active

```
 1  METHOD /iwbep/if_mgw_appl_srv_runtime~get_expanded_entityset.
 2
 3     CASE iv_entity_set_name.
 4        WHEN 'HaulbackHeaderSet'.
 5           TRY.
 6              CALL METHOD super->/iwbep/if_mgw_appl_srv_runtime~get_expanded_entityset
 7                 EXPORTING
 8                    iv_entity_name           = iv_entity_name
 9                    iv_entity_set_name       = iv_entity_set_name
10                    iv_source_name           = iv_source_name
11                    it_filter_select_options = it_filter_select_options
12                    it_order                 = it_order
13                    is_paging                = is_paging
14                    it_navigation_path       = it_navigation_path
15                    it_key_tab               = it_key_tab
16                    iv_filter_string         = iv_filter_string
17                    iv_search_string         = iv_search_string
18                    io_expand                = io_expand
19                    io_tech_request_context  = io_tech_request_context
20                 IMPORTING
21                    er_entityset             = er_entityset
22                    et_expanded_clauses      = et_expanded_clauses
23                    et_expanded_tech_clauses = et_expanded_tech_clauses
24                    es_response_context      = es_response_context.
25              CATCH /iwbep/cx_mgw_busi_exception .
26              CATCH /iwbep/cx_mgw_tech_exception .
27           ENDTRY.
28
29        WHEN 'HaulbackDetailHeaderSet'.
30           copy_data_to_ref(
31              EXPORTING
32                 is_data = gt_haulback_detail_header
33              CHANGING
34                 cr_data = er_entityset ).
35
```

Method	/IWBEP/IF_MGW_APPL_SRV_RUNTIME~GET_EXPANDED_ENTITYSET	Active

```
35
36        WHEN 'HaulbackDetailItemSet'.
37           copy_data_to_ref(
38              EXPORTING
39                 is_data = gt_haulback_detail_item
40              CHANGING
41                 cr_data = er_entityset ).
42
43        WHEN 'EtMessagesSet '.
44           copy_data_to_ref(
45              EXPORTING
46                 is_data = gt_haulback_error
47              CHANGING
48                 cr_data = er_entityset ).
49
50     ENDCASE.
51
52  ENDMETHOD.
```

This method will move back the global table variables, not single structures, to the HTTP response in case we mention them in HTTP GET URL with the expand option. These entities that are retuned back are the ones that have a 1:N relationship with the header.

In case we need to get the return of these tables, we simply call the following URL from Gateway Client:

```
/sap/opu/odata/SAP/YSDSA_HAULBACK_DATAREQUEST_SRV/Haulb
ackHeaderSet?$expand=HaulbackDetailHeaderSet,HaulbackDe
tailItemSet
```

The HTTP XML response will bring these 2 entities sets defined in the URL:

```
+ <link title="HaulbackDetailHeaderSet" type="application/atom+xml;type=feed"
  rel="http://schemas.microsoft.com/ado/2007/08/dataservices/related/HaulbackDetailHeaderSet"
  href="HaulbackHeaderSet('')/HaulbackDetailHeaderSet">
  <link title="HaulbackSurvey" type="application/atom+xml;type=entry"
    rel="http://schemas.microsoft.com/ado/2007/08/dataservices/related/HaulbackSurvey"
    href="HaulbackHeaderSet('')/HaulbackSurvey"/>
+ <link title="HaulbackDetailItemSet" type="application/atom+xml;type=feed"
  rel="http://schemas.microsoft.com/ado/2007/08/dataservices/related/HaulbackDetailItemSet"
  href="HaulbackHeaderSet('')/HaulbackDetailItemSet">
  <link title="HaulbackErrorSet" type="application/atom+xml;type=feed"
    rel="http://schemas.microsoft.com/ado/2007/08/dataservices/related/HaulbackErrorSet"
    href="HaulbackHeaderSet('')/HaulbackErrorSet"/>
+ <content type="application/xml">
 </entry>
```

Conclusion

Now that you are at the end of this book, "*SAP Gateway*", you must have gained valuable and useful insight.

For all developers involved in SAP developments and integrations, I hope this practical guide, that covers the most important aspects of this technology, can help and follow you in your future journey, saving you time with the design, development and troubleshooting.

You are ready to take on the world! :)

Below there is a link of an additional book, that complements this one, that will boost your skills on the SAPUI5 development side.

Here is Wishing You the Very Best on Your Road to Proficiency!

Learn SAP® UI5: The new enterprise Javascript framework with examples

Thank you!

Hope you liked the book and please reread/study it!

Please leave a review in order to help me as an author and to improve and refine the content of this book.

Your review is very important. I will read it very carefully as it will be used as a tool to deliver better books! Many thanks in advance!

Please go to your account on Amazon or click on the link below.

CLICK HERE TO LEAVE A REVIEW ON AMAZON!

Thank you and good luck! Cheers!